The August 17ᵗʰ Realtor
And How to Flourish in The Changing World of Real Estate

By
Ronald B. Fenster

Edited By
Jerold Greenfield

For Information Contact:
Creative Projects International Inc.
info@creativeprojintl.com
www.creativebooks.us

ISBN: 979-8-9878708-2-2
Library of Congress Control Number: 2024944098

Cover Design: Katherine Warden

Dedication

At 78, I can reflect on the bounty of wonderful blessings, opportunities, and adventures life has provided me. My Children: Kevin, Eddie, Renaud, Banesha and Mikael. My Grandchildren: Allison, Jordan, Esme and Camilo. And most importantly my wife, Gigi "Hasta Que La Muerte Nos Separe." I cannot want for anything more.

PROLOGUE

Bob Dylan, had he been a Realtor instead of one of America's most iconic writers and musicians might have penned lyrics for a new song about the Real Estate market and the New NAR Guidelines, "the rules they are a changing." It is not the first time, and it won't be the last.

When announced to the industry, many Realtors zoomed in on what the bottom line was: It was going to be harder to earn their commissions. But they would be wrong because it was going to be much more than how much a Realtor was compensated and how commissions would be regulated.

In the ever-evolving landscape of real estate, professionals are constantly adapting to regulatory changes that impact the industry. This is evidenced by the new guidelines from the National Association of Realtors (NAR), which are aimed at enhancing ethical standards and transparency within Real Estate. They rocked the market by how business will be conducted in the future. These guidelines are not merely regulatory adjustments but are poised to reshape the way realtors conduct business and interact with clients in the future.

Embracing ethical standards are the cornerstone of the new NAR guidelines among real estate professionals and will remain so. These standards are designed to foster trust and accountability within the industry, crucial elements for both clients and Realtors alike. Moving forward, Realtors can expect a heightened emphasis on the three top-of-the-list mandates for success.

Realtors must present transparency, in order to provide clear and upfront communication regarding fees, commissions, and potential conflicts of interest. But it is not just for the Realtors. This transparency aims to empower clients, enabling them to make informed decisions throughout the real estate transaction process.

Professional and professionalism are two words that must touch every function of client contact. Upholding high standards of professionalism in all interactions, including digital and social media platforms, is a focal point. Realtors need to ensure that their online presence aligns with ethical guidelines, maintaining integrity and credibility in the eyes of consumers.

Consumer protection enforcement is integral to all actions. Stricter guidelines surrounding fair housing practices and anti-discrimination policies are enforced rigorously. Realtors need to demonstrate a commitment to diversity and inclusion, promoting equal access to housing opportunities for all.

The future of real estate is increasingly intertwined with technological advancements, and the new NAR guidelines acknowledge this reality. Realtors can anticipate having to master a palette of new concepts and rules.

Digital transformation embraces technology to streamline processes such as virtual tours, electronic document signing, and data analytics. This will become standard practice. Realtors who leverage digital tools effectively with their current successful ways of conducting business can gain a competitive edge. It doesn't mean you have to throw out methods of operation that are working efficiently for you. The combination of the old way and the new can enhance client satisfaction, operational efficiency, and profitability.

Brokerages that are normally responsible for providing your backbone to the internet need to focus more attention on data privacy. With the proliferation of data-driven insights, safeguarding client information and adhering to data privacy laws will be non-negotiable. Realtors and Brokers need to adopt robust cybersecurity measures to protect sensitive data and preserve client confidentiality.

If successfully applied, the new NAR Guidelines will provide increased consumer confidence by promoting transparency and ethical conduct. This heightened trust could lead to more active participation in the housing market, benefiting both buyers and sellers.

As trusted advisors, Realtors will present themselves in a new light and play a pivotal role in guiding clients through complex real estate transactions. To be successful it will no longer work to just fill out a listing agreement or a contract. Beyond the basics, Realtors must rise to a new level of transactional expertise and earn their value for their integrity, market knowledge, and ability to navigate regulatory landscapes.

While the transition to the new NAR guidelines presents challenges, such as adapting to regulatory changes and investing in technology, it also offers numerous opportunities for realtors to differentiate themselves in a competitive market. Those who embrace ethical standards, leverage technology effectively, and prioritize client-centric practices are poised to thrive in the evolving real estate ecosystem. Those who fall short of this new standard of what it means to be a professional Realtor will fall by the wayside.

My conclusion for the successful future for realtors under the new NAR guidelines is one of transformation and adaptation. By prioritizing ethical conduct, embracing technological innovations, and maintaining a client-centric approach, real estate professionals can navigate regulatory changes successfully and build sustainable businesses. As the industry continues to evolve, realtors who proactively embrace change and uphold the highest standards of professionalism are likely to emerge as leaders in a dynamic and resilient real estate market.

But the new conduct of the industry is just half the story. The other half is just like when you received your license and realized that obtaining your license did not teach you much about how you were going to get the work and build a business. That is my story and that is where this book can provide you with insights on how at 60 years old, I launched a new career in Real Estate with only one regret: I did not start sooner.

This book is a roadmap for out of the box ideas that are tried and tested with results that will build your business, build your income, and ethically navigate under any regulations now or in the future. It also provides a path to what I call Community Capture, a concept I developed for myself to become the King of my own community. Wouldn't it be nice one day to walk out your front door and know that all your neighbors know who you are, want to work with you, and know that you are the best Realtor they could turn to when buying or selling?

CHAPTER 1

I wanted a job and picked Real Estate. Did I make a mistake?

By the close of business on my first day as a Realtor I was firm in my conclusion that after studying for and passing my Real Estate Exam I knew next to nothing about this business. What I did know was that my parents Moe and Claire Fenster worked hard to create a home and pay off something called a mortgage. That was about it. Sure, the path to getting a license walked me through the language of Real Estate and it briefed me on the ethical mandates required by my Real Estate Board and the state Real Estate Commission but there was nothing of substance I could recall about how to build a Real Estate business with buyers and sellers. It startled me for a while that I seemed to be going naked into an industry with no skill set to master it. I hoped that my prior career in the television and film business had provided me with the ability to formulate a plan where none previously existed. So, I came up with a plan that 17 years later I can say worked although at the time I developed it, I had grave doubts about success. I no longer have those doubts.

My plan relied on a recollection from my first time at a casino on Paradise Island in the Bahamas. I knew nothing about the game of Craps yet there I was standing at the table placing $5 bets on the green felt boxes. My first several attempts at winning failed and I didn't know why. Well of course I knew why. I did not know the game. Across the table was a short elderly man, his skin darkened from the Bahamian sun. In his hand was a thick cigar. He had the appearance of a man of success who lived the good life. In a way, he was a replica of the Monopoly man. I summed him up to be a winner not only because his dress and comportment presented that image but because his tray was so full of $100 chips that he had to place some of them in the tray next to him. It was obvious that what I did not know about the game he knew many times over. He made large bets dropping chips around the table like large rain drops falling on the green felt lawn. He would also bark out commands to the croupiers regarding the odds he asked for certain bets. I had no flipping idea what he was talking about. It was foreign to me, but the croupiers seemed to know what he meant and scurried to please him. The dice would roll and the chips would flow mainly in the direction of the croupiers. Those bets due the winners were distributed around the table but the bulk of them were pushed across the table to Monopoly Man.

So, after watching for a while and accepting the fact that he knew the game, I placed a $5 chip everywhere he placed a $25 chip. Where he placed a $50 chip or higher, I placed a $10 chip. The dice would roll and after the croupiers cleared the table of the losers' bets and distributed the winnings, I received more money back than I had placed on the table. We did not win every bet but within an hour I had accumulated almost $1,000.

When Monopoly Man decided to cash in, I followed suit. When I think about that experience, I recall two things. First was that Monopoly Man knew how to play the game and knew when to quit while he was ahead. The second thing was that in the scheme of things I considered this to be my first closing where I walked away with money in my pocket.

So, my plan was very simple as I recalled this memory, **Listen to the Voice of Experience and you will succeed.**

This book is written for the new kids on the block regardless of their age and to prepare them for their first day as a Realtor. It is based on my experiences and those of other Realtors who had marshaled their skill set while on the job. These stories repeat themselves every day in our business. When you come across a similar set of circumstances, you will find that more often than not, the only thing that will change are the names, but the stories and their outcomes will be the same.

CHAPTER 2

The New Rules

In early March 2024, just as my editor was about to tell me we were ready to go to the printers, a seismic announcement hit the Real Estate industry that will change the way Realtors conduct their business and are compensated. The first signs of panic set in almost immediately as Realtors across the country tried to figure out how this decision was going to impact their income. As the days rolled on, more information splashed across the internet trying to explain the new rules. Postings from thousands of Realtors predicted doom and gloom in every corner of the industry. Although the new rules will not kick in until August 17th of this year, online chatter could be heard across the country regarding updating resumes and questions were asked by many if they could find another job.

Finally, the dust started to settle, and panic melted into reason and reason produced logical explanations of what these new rules really meant and how the current breed of Realtors would survive and morph into the next iteration.

As a result of the settlement by the National Association of Realtors (NAR), new rules have been established to govern Realtor commissions. The settlement aims to address concerns over anti-competitive practices in the real estate industry and promote transparency and fairness in commission structures.

The settlement prohibits certain anti-competitive practices that were previously common in the real estate industry. This includes rules that limited competition among real estate agents and brokers, such as restrictions on the use of certain technologies or platforms.

Under the new rules, Realtors are required to provide more transparency regarding their commission structures. This includes disclosing how commissions are calculated, what services are included, and any potential conflicts of interest that may arise from the commission arrangement.

Realtors are prohibited from steering clients towards certain properties or services based on the potential commission they would receive. This ensures that clients are provided with unbiased advice and are free to make decisions based on their own preferences and needs. Steering has always been a prohibition but it usually dealt with influencing the ethnic, racial and religious makeup of a neighborhood. Now, it was telling Realtors they could no longer show properties to their clients that would yield them the highest commissions and must show properties with lower commissions also and let the buyer decide what they want to see.

The settlement encourages competition among real estate agents and brokers by removing barriers that may have hindered competition in the past. This includes promoting the use of new technologies and business models that offer alternative ways for consumers to buy and sell real estate.

The settlement establishes mechanisms for enhanced enforcement and oversight to ensure that Realtors comply with the new rules. This may include penalties for non-compliance and regular audits to monitor adherence to the regulations.

Overall, the NAR settlement represents a significant step towards promoting a more competitive and transparent real estate market. By implementing these new rules, consumers can expect greater clarity and fairness in commission structures, as well as increased choice and competition among real estate service providers.

But there is a caveat in all this which reflects on the way a Realtor will deal with buyers and sellers. Sellers will no longer be obligated to pay the buyer's Realtor commission. They can if they so choose but the obligation will default to the Buyer to pay for the buyer's commission. This will be more difficult to master during the change in rules and only the most skillful of Realtors will be able to traverse this buyer obligation. This will most definitely cause a lower negotiated commission and absolutely cause a reduction in the number of full time Realtors. It will most certainly invoke the reshaping of an industry governed by ***Charles Darwin's Survival of the Fittest.***

And it is, all the more important now that if you are to be a successful Realtor that you learn the survival skills I discuss in this book.

Whether your path in Real Estate takes you to Residential or Commercial the basic tenets of how you can grow your business remain the same. Product knowledge is important to hone your skill set. Ethics is equally important in order to navigate your way in an industry laden with the potential to wander from the right path. But most important is the knowledge you receive and the ethics you follow meld together to create a dynamic Real Estate Professional.

There are many more tools in our industry to help guide you than I can discuss because our industry is a foundry of ideas prone to daily change. There are many war stories that I will tell you and many more that have yet to be heard. It doesn't matter if you are 21 or 60. The path to success lays before you and with perseverance the rewards are in plain sight.

CHAPTER 3

Where You Came from and Where You Are Headed

I was close to 60 years old when I took the exam to become a realtor and wondered if I had made the right choice. Two years later after I completed my field training and several closings, I asked myself why I had taken so long. There was no question about loving real estate.

My formal education was in broadcasting and Journalism at the University of Florida. Following four years of living the Gator life, I was awarded an S.I. Newhouse Fellowship in Broadcast Journalism and attended Syracuse University where I received my master's degree. Having interned at WTVJ television in Miami with award winning anchorman Ralph Rennick went a long way towards receiving the Fellowship and I was convinced that my career would continue in the broadcast news industry were it not for a slight detour called the Vietnam War.

After Officer Basic Training at Ft. Gordon, Georgia, I was stationed at the Army Pictorial Center in Long Island City, Queens just across the river from Manhattan.

But shortly after arriving and having signed up for another year of service to receive this choice assignment, the Army closed the Pictorial Center due to inefficiency. My commanding officer addressed the 30 junior officers all of whom had dreams of becoming producers, directors and writers that they would have to put their dreams on hold while they took command of combat platoons. Since I had arrived at the Pictorial Center, I had seen him one time on the day I reported for duty. I recall he had a dour look and did not seem like a happy man. As a matter of fact, he looked like a man who had taken a solemn oath never to smile. But this day was different. As the entire complement of officers piled into the conference room across his face appeared a slight grin of satisfaction just barely hiding his coffee and tobacco-stained teeth pushing through his lips.

Major More, his adjutant announced, "the Colonel has an important announcement for all of you. There have been a lot of rumors swirling about regarding your future assignments and the Colonel is going to set you straight."

"You will all be in Vietnam within six months," he told us quite directly, showing no concern. "CYA!" he shouted.

He was still smiling as he belched the euphemism for the Army's way of saying cover your ass. "Dismissed and good luck," he barked and left the room chuckling down the hallway. All 30 frozen faces roamed the room capturing 30 variations of the same expression. Oh, crap!

My boss in the Special Films Division was a man named Max Kossarin. He was an attorney who did not practice law. After graduating law school, Max had somehow managed to get a job writing scripts for the Bowery Boys comedies which were shot at the pictorial center when it was Paramount studios. For whatever the reasons, he stayed with writing comedies and never returned to law which was my good fortune. He told me that he knew someone in the Pentagon who ran a special operations unit, and he could arrange for an interview, so I jumped on it and within 24 hours I was on the commuter train heading for Washington, DC and the Mothership, The Pentagon. I didn't know much about ~~the~~ mystery unit, but I had been told that it was a hush hush type of unit that worked directly for the Joint Chiefs of Staff.

I met the commanding officer, Colonel Del Vito who greeted me with a smile. He spent about an hour with me and asked me only one question to assess my competence to serve in his command.

"Lieutenant, what is the most important part of film production?" he asked.

I had just read Alfred Hitchcock 's autobiography on the train down to DC and he had mentioned in it that for him, preproduction was the most important part of film production so if it was good enough for Hitchcock, it was good enough for me. I took a stab and bingo, that was what he wanted to hear.

He said to me, "Lieutenant Fenster, you have four choices where we can send you. There is Panama to cover our filmmaking requirements in the southern hemisphere or you can stay at Fort Bragg in North Carolina or you can stay here at the Pentagon in Washington, DC or you can go to Hawaii and cover Asia and Europe."

Well, Panama created a vision very hot and muggy to me, and I remember stories of mosquitoes big enough to feed a family of four. I had taken my basic training at Fort Bragg, NC and I recalled the billboards in and out of Fayetteville with a white horse up on its hind legs. Atop the horse was a man or it could have been a woman but was impossible to tell because a white sheet and hood blocked gender identification. Underneath the horse was a banner that said *"Welcome Brothers You are in Klan Country."* Nope, North Carolina was out of the question. Washington, DC could be a great opportunity and it was close to the second most important broadcast news city in the country, but I heard that it was very expensive to live there on a Second Lieutenant's salary. When I thought of Hawaii only one word came to mind: Aloha. I didn't really think of what it was going to mean to cover Asia and Europe from Honolulu but after spending the winter in New York, I was up for a tan. So, 30 days later I arrived in Honolulu and 21 days after that I was seeing my first six-month tour of combat in Vietnam as a director of a Department of the Army Special Operations Combat Camera Team. For the next two years I roamed Asia and the Pacific documenting subjects of interest to the Department of the Army and on a few occasions The White House.

An exciting tour of duty would be an understatement. My team and I were on a chopper heading into the Parrot's Beak invasion of Cambodia. We rode atop a tank crossing the border into Laos on Operation Lam Son 719. We documented the tiger cages of Vietnamese POW camps and the mortuary procedures of the world's biggest mortuary at Ton Son Nhut Air Base. I even flew from the Mekong Delta to the DMZ with Sammy Davis Jr. documenting his tour of American drug detox centers for our troops hooked on heroin. Davis had been asked by President Nixon to be on the White House Commission on Drug Abuse and the Army wanted to document his tour of Vietnam. I could have lived this adventurous life forever, but when I became eligible to end my tour of duty I put in my papers. I knew there was a very big, classified operation that was going to take place in the near future and my team had been placed on 24 hour notice and I wanted to make that my last production. I had seen enough action and wanted to start my professional career.

Two months after separating from the Army I received a letter from the Lieutenant who replaced me. The operation was no longer secret, having made The Evening News with Walter Cronkite. My team had been on the choppers that landed in North Vietnam to try and rescue American POWs.

When I exited the Army, with what I had seen in Vietnam, I needed a break. I went to Europe and bought a Honda 750cc. It was the first year the model was out, and I followed the sun for three months ending up in Istanbul. At a student pension I was renting, I happened to come across a copy of American Cinematographer magazine and that particular issue was dedicated to filmmaking in Israel. I was only an hour flight away from Israel and had always wanted to go there so I shipped the bike and hopped an El AL flight to the Holy Land.

Three days after I arrived, I met a bunch of film makers who introduced me to Assaf Dayan, General Moshe Dayan 's son. The hero of the Six Day War had a son who opted not to go into the family business but rather become a director and filmmaker.

I thought that not being fluent in Hebrew would relegate me to menial jobs on the film set but we hit it off and he asked me if I was given a script translated into English could I polish it and make it read like American English?

"Yup" and I was now working in the Israeli Film Industry where I stayed for almost two years leaving two days before the start of the Yom Kippur War.

Returning to the US, I grew up in the glamour industry of film, television, computer animation and special effects and it was an exciting vibrant industry with excellent compensation. Working on feature films, television shows, commercials, my production team and I won seven Emmy Awards for computer animation and graphics produced for numerous media events: among them, the opening graphics and animated visual material for the Academy Awards, the Emmys, 7 Super Bowls, the Final Four and Breeders' Cup.

When I left the front of the lens production side of the business, I moved into another incredible challenge, becoming part of the launch team for the PAX Television Network.

I remained at PAX for 7 1/2 years and when the

company was sold and was going to relocate to New York, I decided to stay in Florida and seek work in the only home my family knew. But work did not come quickly. I was now 58 and ageism was starting to creep up in job interviews. Finally, I jumped on an opportunity I thought would be exciting and a lot of fun. I was interviewed for the position of Director of the School of Entertainment and Design Technologies at Miami-Dade college, the largest community college in the country. This really sounded like a feel-good job I could ride into the sunset. Professor Fenster. I liked that.

This department had facilities on four Miami-Dade campuses, and I would be located at the north campus. The income was about half of what I was accustomed to, but it had great benefits and I thought I could readjust our lifestyle to accommodate the cut in pay.

It did not take me long to realize that becoming an instant educator was not going to be easy. In the professional film and television industry writers and producers and directors are all slaves to immediacy in whatever tasks they are trying to accomplish. There are deadlines which must be met and cannot be passed. The entire industry moves on deadlines. Regrettably I found out that in education it's just the opposite, a good idea is discussed to death and then goes to committee discussions to determine how the execution of this idea can be slowed down further. All too often by the time the idea exits the committee it is obsolete. So, I was pretty much in conflict with the administration at the college and constantly fought against putting the brakes on any task I took up. After about a year and a half we parted ways but during that year and a half I studied for and received my real estate license.

I was also working as a consultant on Baby Abuelita, a company my Sister Carol Fenster founded which produced a family of Hispanic heritage dolls that would sing traditional lullabies once you pressed their hands. It was a great Plush toy idea and my sister also wanted to complement the dolls which were flying off the shelves in Walmart and Target and other large brick and mortar stores.   She decided to produce a series of animated Videos. So being the producer, I put together a team of animators from India, sound, and music recording professionals in Miami.

The income from this production supplemented my learning curve as a realtor. Without it, to be honest I'm not sure I would have continued in real estate.

I like to categorize Realtors in three groups young, old, and older. Young Realtors enter the business often right from college or even high school. They are the smallest group. Some become disenchanted with the career; they thought they were destined to serve.

When they get their license, they have two choices to make. To become an independent contractor/realtor working for a Broker or to work for a developer. If I had to do it all over again based on many of the Realtors I've encountered during my career, I would have gone for the developer. First of all, it provides you with a steadier income. You do not have to have a real estate license to work for a developer in their sales office, but it makes sense to get it so that you are prepared to take the next step.

Developers have different means of compensation. You get a much lower percentage of the sales that you make but you have a large inventory provided by the developer. In most cases you work at or near the development. These positions are very difficult to come by, but they can really go a long way to launching a successful real estate career a lot quicker. Some Realtors I know have only done development sales. Others transitioned back and forth.

There's one realtor and I will call him Steve. I met him

when I purchased my own townhome. He was the lead salesperson in the development of 768 units. That's a lot of sales for even a team of Realtors to divide. But it's more than that. Steve had the benefit of capturing every one of his sales as a future legacy sale when the people he sold the home to decide to sell it in the future. That is an incredible list of future business. After the development had sold out and Steve left, he went to a large brokerage in South Florida and remained with them for a while until another opportunity opened for him to sell luxury homes in another community.

Another realtor I had worked with lived in an area near the ocean and was able to land a developer sales position job in a luxury condo on the ocean in sunny Isles. She did not have a license and started as an assistant working her way up to Sales representative. I had purchased a two and a half million-dollar condo from her for a client of mine and we got to know each other well. She had never worked on her own until recently. For the first five years of her career, she worked for one developer after another and compiled an incredible list of clients that she hoped one day would come back to her. They did come back to the extent where she decided to open her own brokerage and focused dealing mainly with her legacy clients on luxury properties. She is doing incredibly well.

As I said these positions are difficult to come by but certainly worth consideration if you're a young entry level or even mid-level realtor.

The second grouping of Realtors I refer to as the Old Realtors. They have successfully navigated their entry into the business, have made a living, and have stayed with it. At one point or another, they find themselves at a crossroad. Do they continue to stay with their broker, or do they get their own Brokers license and venture out on their own? I think their decision will be based on what they defined as their short medium and long-term goals. I remember talking with one of the very successful Realtors in my company and I asked her why with the millions and millions of dollars that she sold every year she didn't go out on her own. Her answer is something for every up-and-coming realtor to consider. She was at the top of her split with the broker. She had thought about starting her own company with her own marquee name, but she had to figure one thing out. She was paying a small percentage of all her sales to the broker and with that percentage in mind her overhead as an independent broker had to be less than her split with her current broker otherwise it just did not make sense. She didn't want to be a large company and have to be responsible for dozens and dozens of Realtors. She could grow her team to the size she felt comfortable managing and avoid most of the overhead she would incur on her own. She didn't want to have to pay a lot of rent and insurance and administrative overhead and larger accounting fees. And every time she put pencil to paper she could not come up with an overhead figure that was less than her current split with her current Broker. So, her decision was to stay with the company and reap the same rewards without creating administrative and overhead headaches.

In the second group, the Old group of Realtors I refer to, split in two directions residential and commercial. Most Realtors who enter the business start off in residential because potential income is more readily available. Commercial deals can take an incredibly long time to consummate. The research is greater, third-party consultations with general contractors and architects may be required and the expenses will be greater. Environmental issues often enter the picture. Whereas the rewards may often be greater the start to finish time to closing is always longer. But either way, the realtor at this time is experienced and has an idea or at least should have an idea of how he wants to build his business. He may stay as an independent single Realtor, or he may decide to join a team. Either way if he's staying in the business after the first 5 to 10 years, he has probably done very well and will continue to do so.

The third 'Older' real estate group also has two subgroups. The first consists of people who have just grown older in the industry. They have been steady producers over the years and by now should be enjoying the rewards of their legacy Clients, people who they've sold or bought for repeatedly. This is something that should be every Realtors goal.

The second 'Older' subgroup are people like me. We are just old. We're not broken. We are not necessarily slowed down by age. We came from other industries and either retired or transitioned out of those industries at an age which is more difficult to allow us entry into other industries. We all assumed that Real estate could be the perfect place to land.

When my job producing the Baby Abuelita videos ended and I jumped into real estate full time, I had made enough progress to feel comfortable. Of course, there was that moment in the Keyes Sudden Success Course taught by Phil Clodgo, a seasoned veteran of Real Estate where he mentioned that the average new realtor made about $14,000 a year. I thought I had made a terrible mistake. But at the end of my first year, I had made nearly $40,000 as a part time Realtor and so I convinced myself that I could be a hotshot. The next year I shot right to a six-figure salary. It was still not where I wanted to be, but I was on the road to success. Since then, I never looked back and never regretted the move and if anything would always kick myself for not moving into real estate sooner.

As I write this book, I'm 78 years old in pretty good

health with only one heart attack having nothing to do with real estate. I have no intention of finding a green bench to retire. Real Estate gives me a sense of purpose and as a grandfather it gives me a great sense of joy every time, I find a new young couple with children looking to purchase their first home. I also know that I am building a legacy for my brand. One of my sons, Kevin is a firefighter, and is also a member of my team. His dream was always to be a firefighter and with the schedule that firefighters keep, he has enough time to have real estate as his second profession. Once I am no longer able to do real estate, the legacy clients that I created over the years will fall to him.

One of best things that a Realtor can hear when he answers the phone is someone saying, "Hi, remember me? You sold us our first house and we want to sell it and find a larger one." That is what building your legacy business is all about and it should always be top of mind as you build your business.

In this my 17th year practicing Real Estate, I would say that at least 50 % of my business is from former clients. When you think about how hard it was for you to start and get to your first few contracts, attaining this mix of new and old clients is where you want to be.

CHAPTER 4

The Table Where the Cool Kids Sit

Remember when you were in grade school, there was always a table in the cafeteria where the cool kids ate. You either ate at the table or wanted to eat there. If you had a game plan, it was to someday, somehow be invited to the cool table. Most of us were content to remain in our own circle and move at our own pace.

Selecting a Broker was similar with one big difference, every Broker claims to be the Cool Kid at the Lunch Table. I skipped lunch the day I selected my Brokerage. I did have conversations with two other Brokers after passing my Real Estate License Exam, but they reached out to me. They were large companies, but I was not familiar with them. They presented themselves to me as full service with everything I would need to learn about becoming a successful Realtor. But there was one Real Estate Office I wanted to explore before all the others. Keyes Real Estate was a company with name recognition. Growing up on Miami Beach in the 1950's, I would see their signs everywhere and here we were in 2006 and I was still seeing their yard signs. As a business professional, that meant something to me. The company had withstood the test of time. And there was an office less than a quarter mile from my home. It was an easy paced walk, so I took the walk to find out why they were still in business.

When you get your license, you get two things: An envelope in the mail and an onslaught of phone calls from Cool Table Brokerages inviting you to join them. I suffered endless calls and only engaged two recruiters. By the time I walked into the Keyes office, I was told that the company offered their new Realtors an incredible training program and their mentor program allowed Realtors to shadow experienced Realtors who were designated field trainers. As time progressed with Keyes which was a family-owned Brokerage steeped in the history of Miami real estate, I discovered from other Realtors that many of the smaller companies only provided instruction on a catch as catch can basis and that you would have to go to Realtor Board training seminars to play catch up and expand your knowledge. Without intense initial and ongoing training and a mentor program, most newbies will find themselves dead in the water and get discouraged very quickly.

If asked today, as a new kid on the block, would I join a small brokerage or a large one, I would say three things: First, join a Broker with the resources to provide a continuing and intense education program with an ongoing mentoring program. It does not have to be a national company with offices all over the US.

Second, after your education is sufficient and you feel comfortable maneuvering without the training wheels, it will be easier for you to decide to remain at your initial brokerage or interview with other Brokers who might best suit your goals going forward.

Third, and this may sound strange, but the last thing you need to worry about is the money you are going to earn in your first year. Believe me, if you lay out a good business plan, the fruits of your labor will start to pay off the second year and every year thereafter.

Most large brokerage firms will assign you to a trainer or mentor. And do not be shocked that you will have to compensate your mentor with a portion of your first few sales. If your mentor is good, it is the best money you can spend. If you don't think your mentor is giving you the time you need, talk to your broker, and ask for a new mentor. It happens, so don't be shy about asking.

When I joined Keyes, which at the time had about 25 offices throughout the southeast Florida coast, I was struck by the management's trickle-down concerned interest in my success as one of their Realtors. When I finally was introduced to Ted Pappas, the Chairman and his sons, Mike and Tim, it was like a family gathering. I had just met them at a company function and yet, after having an opportunity to talk with them, I felt that I had known them for a long time. Later, I met Christina Pappas, Mike's daughter. She was sitting in a cubicle in the Coral Gables office as I observed her doing what every Realtor is supposed to do, making calls and learning the business from the ground up. It made me think of my Dad and working in his wholesale grocery business. I learned everything about it from sweeping the floors in the warehouse to riding shotgun on the delivery trucks making their appointed rounds at all the hotels and restaurants on Miami Beach. Evidently, Christina honed her craft well because 15 years later, she is now President of the company leading over 3,000 Realtors into a new generation of the real estate industry.

My last corporate position in the television industry was as Vice President of a public company and the words 'concern and warmth' did not exist. But at Keyes, I knew I would be comfortable and 17 years later, I am still convinced I made the right choice.

Chapter 5

Picking your Brokerage

When I passed my state license exam, I was elated that at 60 years old, I was able to embark on a new career. My prior accomplishments in the film, video and television industries had come to a screeching halt in part due to ageism. Those industries had always been prone to looking for talented new blood and the unspoken definition of "new blood" was youth. At 60, I felt like I had fallen into an abyss that kept spinning out of control and would not let me escape. It was like a riptide current which sucks you in the opposite direction you want to swim.

They say that when you are caught in a riptide you should go with the flow and try to escape in the direction it is pulling you. So, after numerous attempts at relocating myself in an industry that was very good to me, I decided to go with the flow and see if I could escape in a new direction.

I knew it was going to be tough. My career had bestowed seven Emmy awards on the company I founded and helped to herald in the age of digital video technology. After exiting my company, I was hired to help launch the PAX Television Network which was an opportunity few people can experience. When PAX was sold, the new owners decided they were no longer going to produce original television content and with that decision, I found myself on the ever-increasing list of competent yet still talented old folks.

But it was not a bee line from PAX to the real estate

industry. To be honest, I still felt there was something out there for me that would take advantage of my abilities as a creative director and producer. I had made a list of all the potential careers that my life experience qualified me for, and real estate was not one of them. I never considered it a creative entity and I longed for creative challenges. Later on, I would realize that only through creativity can a Realtor be successful. I just did not want to give it the chance.

Continuing to follow the flow my path led me to Miami Dade College, the largest community college in the country with five campuses and over 100,000 students. They had a film and television department and my resume screamed out that I was the right person to become the Director of the School of Film and Television. The position had been a revolving door of academic type directors and the thought was maybe an industry professional might help the school achieve the desired goals.

I jumped at the opportunity but after a year at the helm I concluded that I wasn't going to be able to accomplish the school's goals under the operating conditions that were mandated by the college and my thoughts changed to the realm of what is next? I was not old enough to retire and I felt that I had much too much energy to find a perch in front of a fishing hole.

My list of opportunities was growing smaller and after several passes, I decided to give real estate a try. I never talked to anyone about it and I am glad I didn't. If the person I talked to had presented a negative view I probably would not have given it a try. I don't want to discourage anyone reading this book but if I was honest, I would tell a prospective real estate applicant something to the effect of: It is hard, very hard. You might work six months without earning your first commission check. Maybe longer. Maybe never. Don't look for a salary, there are few opportunities with only salaries. Don't look for benefits. There are few companies which provide benefits. Don't look for a company that is going to provide clients who are guaranteed to give you listings and sales. The most you can expect are leads but when you find out what the definition of a lead is, you won't like that either.

What you will find out is that any success you achieve will be based on your own initiative, your own ability, and your own resourcefulness.

So, I made the decision to try real estate, but I was fortunate to have picked a time that would allow me to earn an income while I took the exam, select a brokerage to join and craft a plan to launch my new career.

As I said, I was fortunate to have an opportunity to take on a freelance production contract to produce a series of children's animated videos based on a new toy called Baby Abuelita. My sister, Carol, had founded the company which produced dolls for the Hispanic market. The dolls were a cute caricature of an Abuela and Abuelo, the endearing names children called their grandparents. The dolls were a great success and a grade school curriculum had also been designed to support the cultural relationships in the Hispanic family unit. The videos were designed for the home market and for television. I produced the animation in India and all the music and postproduction came together in Florida.

This opportunity allowed me to enter real estate while still earning a good income and that was important to me. Now, as a field trainer, I can reflect on many of the trainees I have worked with who jumped into the business without the means to support themselves until the commissions started to flow. Part time jobs were of little help and the time spent usually interfered with the necessary day time hours required in Real Estate. Given the choice, jumping into the business full time is the recommended way to go but not always available to every new Realtor.

As you can imagine, working for a time with no visible income can weigh very heavily on you and challenge your career decision. There are very few industries which do not offer some form of compensation even if it is minimal during your training. Even the armed forces might have you digging ditches and running miles in the mud in darkness to increase your stamina but at least they're still paying you. Not real estate!

When will I get my first listing, my first sale, my first anything that will put food on the table or pay my mortgage? You convince yourself that it is just around the corner. But you need money and so you start to increase your hours at your day job and take more and more time away from working on your business plan. After a while, without seeing the fruits of your labors, you get closer to throwing in the towel.

So along with your plan to become a Realtor, my advice is to formulate a corresponding plan that addresses how you are going to support yourself or at least contribute to your family income while you are in the formative training period.

Undoubtedly, the best way is to always jump in with both feet and start on day one as a full-time Realtor. Most part time Realtors work during the day and stumble into the office late in the day when most of the full time Realtors are out in the field showing homes. In today's new reality due to the COVID-19 effect on the traditional office workplace the jury is still out if the traditional in office work environment will ever return to days of yore. I cannot speak for other Brokers, but at my Keyes office, the return to the traditional office culture is rapidly returning and that is significantly important.

I bring this up because most of the knowledge I absorbed, I received in the office. Real estate offices are typically divided into small open spaced cubicles which do not allow for a lot of privacy. So, conversations are always spilling over and it is not uncommon to hear the essence of other people's deals communicated via the phone or directly with other Realtor's clients who are in the office. You become a sponge soaking up the sound bites of other Realtors' deals, problems, and negotiating strategies. The office is the place you want to be, and you can't be there if your most productive hours of the day are spent elsewhere. The office to a Realtor is like the hive to a bee with one exception. A bee's goal is to pollinate outside the hive and bring his work product to the hive. A Realtor gets pollinated in the hive and takes his work product outside. More hours in the office will equate to how quickly you achieve success.

But what else goes on in the office that can help you make that first deal? That depends on the Brokerage you select to hang your license. In Florida, and I assume in most if not all states, a Realtor Associate, the entry level licensed classification, must work through a Brokerage. What distinguishes one Brokerage from another is the character of its ownership and management and the tools it provides the Realtors who operate under its banner. The thing about a Brokerage is that it cannot hide the good, the bad, or the ugly. Everything dealing with the way a Brokerage has conducted its business is accessible for review in public records, social media, and the least exacting sort of review, what you hear on the streets. Before you decide to sign on to a brokerage check their reviews. Check to see if there were complaints lodged against them with your state's Department of Business and Professional Regulation. Even go so far as to find the names of their leading Realtors and check their reviews. It will be well worth the time and provide a lot of comfort once you make your final decision.

Let me address the issue of available tools first. There is a myriad of all sorts of canned training software, but in my experience in person classroom training is the best which allows for an interchange of experiences from fellow Realtors. But that takes a Brokerage that has an education or training department. In many smaller brokerages there is often not the depth of personnel to support this requirement on an ongoing basis. The financial ability to support a full-time training department is much more challenging and the personnel available are more on a catch as catch can basis.

I want to make it clear that I am not beating up on small brokerages. Quite the contrary. It does not mean that a small brokerage should be dismissed as being inferior but in all the firsthand cases I am personally aware of is that you learn and work more on your own in a smaller brokerage and that is okay once you have become a veteran Realtor.

My advice is to take advantage of what a larger Brokerage can offer you as a new entry level Realtor Associate. There is a comradery available that in most cases you will miss in a smaller brokerage.

And so now you ask, how do I find the brokerage that is right for me? Don't worry, the moment you pass your state license exam, your phone will start ringing from company recruiters asking you to come into their office to meet with the Broker or recruiter. They will usually give you some attractive information about their company to encourage you to set up an interview. Select the ones which you are most impressed with and make the appointments.

When you arrive, have a few questions prepared and use that same list of questions for all the brokers you meet. When I did my interviews, I selected three companies and below are the questions I asked:

1. How will your company provide me the training I need to become a successful Realtor?
2. How will I receive my initial and ongoing training?
3. Do you have a mentorship program and if so, will I have an opportunity to interview with a few mentors?
4. How does your brokerage split the commissions with your Realtor Associates and what is the path to increasing those splits?

Note that I did not ask a question about how much I was going to receive in the form of commissions. I already knew that from reading about the real estate industry. That figure is memorialized in the Multiple Listing Service (MLS) section on commissions if you are acting as a buyer's agent. If you are representing the seller, you and your client determine what the commission will be.

The question is, therefore, what portion of the commission which goes to your brokerage is going to you and what portion the Broker is going to retain. And herein is the single most often repeated error a new Realtor makes when it comes to selecting a Broker.

When it comes to your commission remember this formula:

100% of Zero = Zero.

It doesn't matter what the split is between you and the brokerage you select if you do not bring in business. I have never come across a Broker who during your training period offers a generous commission split. More important is to ask what tools your Broker will provide that will help you plan a roadmap to success. After a reasonable amount of time learning the ropes and demonstrating that you can generate business you can always negotiate a better split than you first agreed to receive. Always! And I say this without reservation: Once you have demonstrated that you are an income producing Realtor, if your current Broker does not recognize this and decides not to reward you for your success, consider placing your license elsewhere. You will not have a problem finding a brokerage that will review your potential, which is no longer bluster but reality with a history of closings to prove it. But realize that the commission split is not and should never be the only reason you might want to change Brokerages and I will get into that later.

Brokerages come in all shapes and sizes and vary widely on the support they can provide their Realtors. My Broker, The Keyes Company, has vast resources to provide its Realtors. I am not writing an advertisement for Keyes but I have to use this company as a model example because it is the only Brokerage I have worked for and it has provided me everything I have needed from my first day to the present. There are many other brokerages that I am sure can provide the tools you need but describing what Keyes offered me will give you an idea of what you should look for in the selection of your Brokerage.

Their continuing education resources both in the classroom and on-line are extensive and they spend an enormous amount of money to provide these resources. Smaller companies may not have the same financial resources and may be more suitable for Realtors who already have experience.

Over the years, Keyes has created a family of services such as a mortgage company, a title company, an insurance company, a property management company, and a relocation company.

All these companies provide training and keep you immediately up to date on changing rules and regulations in their sectors of the industry. I like to think of them as guardians of the road to a successful closing.

I don't use them for every deal because sometimes your client will dictate who they want to use for a mortgage, title, or insurance company but collectively, they are part of the spine that adds strength to the overall services provided.

All boards of Realtors provide training to their members, but larger brokerages have the financial resources to provide their own training on a continuing basis. Much of this training is proprietary and is only available at considerable expense to your Broker. Providing this training makes a significant statement that your Broker will support you and is not reluctant to invest their money in your training.

All Brokerages to some degree subscribe to lead subscription services that help their Realtors identify potential buyers and sellers. Whether it is the broker or a third-party resource who tells you they will provide you with guaranteed qualified leads, understanding the word "lead" has a very nebulous and often confusing meaning. A third-party lead generation company such as Zillow, Trulia, or Realtor.com, is going to charge you a subscription or per lead fee. My history in the business of converting leads to contracts has been highest when I generated my own leads by using my sphere of influence, door knocking, or staging events.

I also mentioned the character of the company as a consideration and that is extremely important. Remember that any industry has buzz word names for the leading companies. The company does not have to be the biggest in your market but it should have name recognition and for all the right reasons.

Companies often must work years to achieve positive name recognition. A company can achieve a tarnished reputation very quickly. The company you want to go with should always be one with a good reputation that has withstood the test of time. Your research can easily determine which one is right for you. My advice is that regardless of the incentives a brokerage might offer you, consider cautiously joining a company that may not have the best reputation.

A Brokerage's product is the ability to provide ethical, professional, and knowledgeable real estate service to its customers by employing well trained Realtors who abide by a strict code of conduct. To be considered at the top of its game, it can sell nothing less. Once that reputation has been tarnished it is difficult if not impossible to recover. So, take the necessary time to assess your possibilities and choose wisely.

In my early years on numerous occasions, I found myself at the foot of an ethical bridge I had to cross. On one side there I stood wanting to cross the bridge but standing guard and blocking me was another Realtor who presented a requirement that had to be fulfilled if I were to be allowed to cross. Usually, it involved money in the form of a kickback. Representing a Buyer, it was structured something like this, "If you want me to recommend you get the contract, are you going to take care of me?" the Realtor would say. There was never an email or text. It was always in person with a wink and a nod. Yes, it was that blatant. Once I recalled, it went the other way when I was the listing agent where the Buyer's Realtor said, "I'll give you 25% of my commission if you award me the contract."

If you feel that you have been placed in a compromising position there is only one word you can possibly muster up in response, "No." Your guiding light should be this question: "Am I a Realtor who will do anything for a deal or am I a Realtor who is going to ethically build a business he can be proud of and a shining light for others to aspire to."

Instead of trying to cross that bridge with a Realtor who would make that offer just ignore it and find another way. Do not be shy about contacting the Realtor's Broker and reporting him. If the Broker tries to minimize the ethical violation, that would certainly be a name to add to your list of Brokers you should never work with. And if you encounter incidents like I have described, let your broker know of it.

The character of the Brokerage you work for is everything and it helps make your efforts listing and selling homes easier. It is an important business obligation to yourself that you make it clear to Realtors and Brokers you are working with that you are working for a company that would never put you or them in an unethical and compromising position.

So, ask other Realtors and Brokers about companies with the best reputations and hang your hat on their door. You can't go wrong when your competition tells you with conviction that the company you have decided to work with is an excellent choice.

CHAPTER 6

The First Deal

So here I was in a class of about 30 wannabe Realtors. We were listening to Phil Clodgo who from the moment he started talking exuded a statesmanlike persona. If he was not a Real Estate educator, he could have easily been mistaken for an ambassador. His comportment was friendly and warm, and he presented his initial explanation of what was involved in becoming a Realtor in an exciting manner which would not put you to sleep. I was already nearly 60 years old and almost anything could put me to sleep but I could see that Phil was not going to be one of them. Everything he discussed had a ring of authority and authenticity I suppose based on years of being in the RE trenches himself. If you have a good speaker, war stories can be very interesting.

Phil paused and asked each of us to take a minute and explain what our current or prior professions were and why we wanted to become Realtors. The unanimity of the responses centered around wanting to make more money. There was the attorney who by his own admission confessed that he was not very good at the profession and hoped that real estate would be better for him. I recall two hairdressers who wanted to better provide for their families. There was a chef who had a bad kitchen accident and needed to take a break. But all of them came back to the same basic theme of improving their lives while making money and being their own boss. Years later I thought about that group and wondered how many of them had achieved their dream.

We were scheduled for eight days of Phil's Sudden Success class with practical information and exercises the license study course did not cover. After the introductions, Phil formally launched into his class. Things started to make sense and from all appearances, the product nature of Real Estate started to integrate into basic tenants of being a salesperson. I had been a salesperson all my life. Not the Fuller Brush type, but the film and television type, always needing to sell my creative concepts by creating personal relationships. It was Dale Carnegie, the master guru of all sales gurus who said, that "Sales is giving your client enough information about your product to convince him that he is justified in buying it."

What I needed from Phil was product knowledge. The sales portion I was well versed in from my prior career where salesmanship was the only way to marshal technicians, creative directors, writers, art directors, actors and a myriad pastiche of other crafts and services to show up on the same day and integrate each of their jobs to create a concerto which moved the film or show to a successful completion. When things went well, it was the initial salesmanship which set the course of success. When they did not go well, it was salesmanship which steered the ship back on course.

So, you are asking what does that have to do with real estate? Remember what it is you are selling. It is yourself! If selling yourself along with your product knowledge, your ethical approach to real estate is not firmly etched into your client's perception of you, you will fail to make the sale.

Your presentation will have everything to do with the success of selling yourself. Ask your closest friends to critique your presentation as a salesperson, especially if English is a second language. In my 17 years, I have had many students who came from different countries and spoke with a very thick accent affecting the clear enunciation of their English. In South Florida, this is particularly prevalent and many Realtors retreat to their native tongue to conduct business because they may be embarrassed to speak English. But that may limit the pool of potential clients you try to service. My advice here is stop and get off that bus. If you need to get help with your accent, there are many avenues you can explore. No, I'm not a speech therapist but there is not a day where I do not have difficulty understanding potential clients and other Realtors. Part of the reason, to be honest, is that I'm now 78 years old and have started to lose my hearing and although I can compensate with the use of hearing aids, it is not the loudness of the voice that I hear but the quality of the speech. And I find myself over and over asking the speaker to repeat themselves.

So how do you tactfully tell your trainee that you can't understand him? And that they need to improve their diction. I use a fun method but first I must be totally honest with the student. I tell them "I'm sorry, student, but I am having difficulty understanding you. Can we talk about it?" That usually breaks the ice, and we discuss options to improve their language skills. So, what is the fun part? I tell them about a Hollywood film clip from a very famous movie called My Fair Lady with Audrey Hepburn and Rex Harrison. There is a scene where Audrey, who was self-described as a street urchin and the daughter of a chimney sweep, lets loose with her terrible Cockney accent. She is confronted by the good doctor, Rex Harrison, and Colonel Pickering, a friend of his and a speech expert. They get Audrey to recognize that her communication skills are terrible but can be changed. They do it by putting to song a commonly known phrase, "the rain in Spain falls mainly on the plain." Stumbling at first, she tries to mimic them in song and fails terribly. But she doesn't give up and tries and tries again, which of course is the lesson -- do not give up on yourself. As she progresses, you can hear the Cockney accent fade away and the clear English accent emerge. Well, of course this is a movie, and it is fiction, and it is not going to happen in one choral sitting.

Over the years, as I would pass my students in the office, I would chant "the rain in Spain" and hear them answer back in song "falls mainly on the plain" and know that their improvement was ongoing and most definitely better. Remember, your communication skills are the keys to your success. To settle into complacency and shortchange yourself is to shortchange your long-term success.

After the first few days of Sudden Success, Phil set us up with a practical exercise. He gave each student a set of phone numbers which represented FSBO's (For Sale By Owner). Once you have been plying your trade, you become instantly aware that homeowners who try to sell their homes on their own have one thing in common and they are not shy about telling you, "We don't need a Realtor to sell our home." If you ask why, they will tell you, "All you are interested in is the commission." Well, yes, that's true I thought. It is compensation for my efforts on your behalf, a concept in existence since Biblical times. It is surprising how many people you will meet in this business who think otherwise. If you try to explain that to a hostile homeowner, you are wasting your time. There are other ways to deal with that situation and I will get to those later.

So, the rules of the exercise were simple. Everyone was to call the numbers on their sheet until they were able to set up a listing appointment. The first person who got an appointment was the winner and would receive $100 in marketing dollars to purchase swag from the Keyes online marketing website.

Now, normally this would be an easy exercise, but Phil gave us some background information on the current state of the market. It was 2006 and home prices were escalating to ridiculous levels and the first wave of foreclosures was starting to sweep the market. Very few Realtors were aware that the winds of fraud were starting to blow across the nation. People were easily getting mortgages they could not possibly have qualified for a year earlier. Down the road many of them would experience the harshness of foreclosure. In many cases, the experience of losing their home would rip families apart and right in the middle of it would be a Realtor who had to work with the bank that was foreclosing on their home. The banks were most definitely perceived as the bad guys and the Realtor part of the gang who profited from selling their homes. In addition to the banks, many buyers in this period of turmoil were large institutions and private investors who gobbled up the lower priced properties of a market which had peaked and then crashed with a thunderous clap. Individuals wanting to step up to larger homes were cashing in on their existing homes and purchasing new ones but at extremely high prices that seemed to make no sense. They thought there was sustainability in the market and that the good times would roll on forever.

Real Estate is part of the financial world and in that world memories of the past are catalogued by large investment companies looking to retain information for future investments. But for the individual, those memories tend to fade as time passes. And by 2007 memories of the prior stock market tech crash were all but forgotten. Sellers of homes who received ridiculous sums of money self-anointed themselves as financial geniuses. Had they stopped and given some thought to what they were about to do, they might have saved themselves from losing their new homes. Regrettably, many did not and with their newly anointed self-educated financial knowledge of the real estate market, they started investing in real estate taking the money they made from their first sale and spreading it across purchases in a declining and short sale market.

If you're a new Realtor you may not even be aware of the term short sale. I certainly was not but learned about it quickly because that was the market condition when I became a Realtor. In a short sale situation, the homeowner is underwater with their mortgage and owes more than the house is worth. The homeowner asks the bank for permission to short sell the property for less than it's worth. The owner still owns the home during the sale process, but the bank or lending institution must give permission for the sale to be consummated. The owner still owes the bank for the shortfall which becomes a loss for the owner. If the bank forgives the shortfall, it registers with the IRS as a taxable gift. When the market crash first started, the IRS forgave the loss but there was only a short window and after the window expired, if you bought a home with a mortgage of $600,000 and sold the home with only $400,000 to pay toward the mortgage company you still owed the mortgage company $200,000. If the mortgage company forgave that short fall, the IRS could tax the $200,000 as a gift. So many people initially who short sold their homes did not have to suffer additional injury by then having to pay the IRS. But as time went on the IRS dropped the forgiveness and more pain was added to the sale of losing the home.

Just as in the tech crash of the 1990's, where stockbrokers and financial advisors drank their own bathwater and invested huge commission gains into more IPO's that flooded the market and suffered high losses, Realtors were being lured into buying homes for themselves thinking they could flip them in a short period of time and make quick money. And for a period, they did and with each successive sale they took self-pleasure in convincing themselves that they were geniuses. They bragged to their colleagues of the latest plays they made and the colleagues listened and wanted in. Remember when I said that the best advice you can get is from an experienced Realtor. Please do not count this time as one of those eras of good advice.

Appraisals were all over the place and valuations just made no sense. Everyone was becoming amateur appraisers establishing buy and sell prices that defied logic. Few of us could really understand what was going on. Especially those of us who were newly licensed. We looked to the voice of experience and in many cases the voice of experience was itself and at that time and under those circumstances incredibly inexperienced.

With my first call from Phil's list, I was about to experience the short sale market by getting a listing that defied the logic of that time. I retreated to a corner of the room and said to myself, "Okay, Dale Carnegie, let me see what I can recall from your sales course. Start dialing."

I started crunching numbers into my cell phone. Call one did not answer. Same as call two and three. By the time I got to my fourth call, I could hear others in the room starting conversations. With one ear I listened for my phone call to connect and with the other ear I listened to hear if others were connecting and starting their pitch for a listing appointment. Call five, nothing. Six and a voice.

"Hello," I said. "Is this Mr. Stills?

"Yes," a friendly voice responded. Great, he was not hostile. At least not yet.

"Mr. Stills," I continued. "My name is Ron Fenster and I am a Realtor with Keyes Real Estate. I see that you have your home for sale."

I could hear his voice tighten as he asked me if I was a buyer or "just one of those Realtors?"

It was the moment of liftoff. Every bit of confidence I could conjure up within five seconds was on the launchpad. My rocket ship had a mission. It was to disarm a potentially hostile client who could end my sales pitch with a simple click of the phone.

"I am proud to say, I am a Realtor but I'm not sure if as you say, I am one of *those* Realtors. By the way, what would I have to do to be one of those? I mean if your opinion is that those Realtors are only interested in earning a commission than I guess I won't disappoint you. But you know, no Realtor can earn a commission unless they sell your home and that is what you are interested in right?"

"Well of course but I can do it myself. Why do I need you?" he shot back.

"You don't need me per se," I responded. I think I shocked him with my response.

"Then why are you calling me?"

"Because I agree with you. Sooner or later, you may be able to sell your home but at what price and how long will it take? And of course, I want to earn a commission, but I only earn it if I am successful and can sell your house quickly for the net amount you want to put in your pocket. Does that make sense? Look, at this point, I don't know what your goals are, how quickly you want to sell or anything else about what you want to accomplish. All I'm asking for is ten minutes of your time. Can we set a time I can come over with my research and marketing plan?"

His answer just told me I won. "I guess so, but I know what my home is worth, my neighbor listed his house, and it is the same as mine and he put on the market for $425,000."

"And he sold it? How long did it take?"

"Well, no, not yet. But I'm sure he will. Zillow says it is worth what he is asking." The agony of the word Zillow at that time was new to me and I sloughed it off. Later it would become a thorn in my side as it did for most Realtors when potential sellers would quote Zillow valuations as if they were a messenger from the gods.

"And Zillow has been in your house to see it?" I asked.

There was a pause as if he was thinking about my question. So, I continued. "And has Zillow been in your house to see some of the improvements you have made during your ownership?"

"No they haven't" he said as if coming to a realization.

"Then Zillow might be underestimating the value of your home. I'll tell you what. I'm free tonight and I don't live far from you. If you can give me those ten minutes I asked for, I will show up with the research that will answer all your questions and concerns."

"Okay, I guess I can spare ten minutes."

I exchanged a few other pleasantries, then hung up. "Phil." I stood up wondering what the research was that I was going to show him. "I have an appointment." There was a sly smile spreading over the face of my newly appointed Oracle of real estate.

About the research? I had been a Realtor for less than six weeks and it just hit home to me that I had no research. I had no technique on how to make a presentation for a listing. What I was sure I had was this success of a sales call coupled with a huge ditch I had just dug for myself. I was full of adrenaline from the success of my first call...well, actually my sixth. But what mattered was that I did it and I thought I was now a hot Realtor. I was on the way to my first listing. My first commission. Watch out, Real Estate world. Ron Fenster is now walking among you. Little did I know what lay ahead. Everything was going to be put in motion and everything was going great unless through my inexperience the whole thing fell apart. But I wasn't going to let it. I had an experienced mentor, and I was going to drag him along with me to my listing appointment.

Trainers are assigned. They become Mentors when the guidance they give you is successfully applied. When I first started at Keyes I was assigned a Trainer. He never made it to being my mentor and I just felt from the start that we did not click so I did what I advised you earlier, I asked my broker for a change and he gave me a Realtor who was very knowledgeable and popular among his colleagues. His name was Marco Zarfati.

That afternoon, I returned to my office elated and eager to tell Marco that I won Phil's FSBO contest and we had our first listing appointment that night. I should have called him because I made the appointment without knowing if he was going to be available.

When I told him, I was relieved to find out that he was available. He was also excited that this success happened so quickly, because it usually doesn't. We had about two hours to get our research done and prepare a listing appointment book. I didn't have a clue at the time what this would require so I would ride the coattails and the depth of Marco's experience. He had me watch and ask questions as we looked for similar listings and sales and prepared a booklet which showed how the resources Keyes had at its disposal would assist in capturing the listing and prepare for sale of the home. Once the listing book was completed, I was impressed and felt we were destined to rock and roll.

We showed up at the house on time and met with the owners, Ken and Rita. They were in their late 30's and had decided to sell their home and move to Denver. Rita was able to relocate through her company and was going to start her new job in two months and Ken was confident he was going to be able to get a job in his field. They had already made a recon trip to the Denver area and fell in love with a new home and placed a deposit on it. I thought at the time this information was crucial in convincing them that they were on a short timeline to sell. I wasn't aware of it at the time because this was my first listing appointment and the first time I'd heard the phrase "I don't have to sell." Usually shouted at Realtors by sellers, it was rarely true. They did have to sell. And with a new job ready to start, Rita's schedule left no time for delays. Their home had already been on the market for 60 days. If they didn't discuss it in our pitch time, I was sure Marco would bring it up.

We were given a tour of the house and with an exchange of body language it appeared Marco and I agreed that the house was very plain with no remarkable upgrades. I could not imagine why anyone would pay $425,000 for it. It did have a pool squeezed into a small yard with lots of weeds. There was no hurricane protection which is important in Florida to get a much better insurance rate for the homeowner's hurricane protection. There was no curb appeal. The Stills had paid $240,000 about five years earlier. They had determined somehow by using Zillow and what their neighbors told them that they were going to be able to sell at $425,000 without a Realtor. Their expectations were in hog heaven but the reality of what they were going to face was considerably less. Their new home in Denver was going to cost them $500,000 and they needed the accumulated equity in their current home to afford the new one.

We all sat down in the living room and Marco began what would become the first of a thousand pitches I would experience in the years to come. Because this was my first listing agreement, I was mesmerized by Marco's polished style.

Very few Realtors went from the cradle to their Real Estate license unless they were born into a Real Estate family. Most new Realtors will have had a history of other employment prior to Real Estate. Marco's was colorful. He was born in Italy. His father was a singer and left Italy at an early age to sing his way across South America. The family eventually came to the US and entered the restaurant business. Marco became the chef and his dad would entertain the patrons singing Italian songs. His dad once told me that they had a pact between them that if Marco did not poison the patrons with his cooking, he would soothe them with his voice. I guess the pact worked well for several years. I did have the chance to taste Marco's cooking, which was excellent, and to hear his dad's voice, which I recall was exceptional. He was in my opinion right up there with Pavarotti.

I think being in the restaurant business can groom you to charm people and Marco had a magical ability to charm. As I watched him wind his way through the presentation, I could see that some of the initial owner hesitation I witnessed when we entered the house had subsided and the owners were becoming engaged seriously in what Marco was saying. So was I.

One of the things that Dale Carnegie reminded salespeople to do was to ask for the order. Don't assume that because you fulfilled the necessity to convince the client that they have enough facts to justify buying your product that they are going to jump up and shout, "I'm sold. Where do I sign?"

But occasionally they actually do. In this case, Ken stood up at the conclusion and asked if he and his wife could have a moment and he led her out to the pool. They returned in a few minutes and asked two questions. The first was how long did we think it would take to sell their home and did we think that the asking price was realistic? Marco told them that the first question would be dictated by the second. He explained that a home priced right sells quicker and, in our opinion, we thought that the current asking price was higher than the comps dictated. We left the current condition of the house out of consideration. Marco would later discuss with them some ideas to better stage the house for sale. And of course, they wanted to know if we could work with them on the commission. Marco had some good answers to address the commission. I kept my eyes on the sellers to see if I could detect their acceptance. The husband showed positive body language responses, but the wife seemed less accepting.

Up to this time, I had been the fly on the wall observing, reluctant to interrupt Marco, but here was something I thought I could insert that would make them think of the main goal, selling this home and moving to their new home and new life in Colorado.

"If I may add to what Marco is saying, we have to keep your goal in the forefront of all your considerations. You have a timeline to start work in Colorado and close on your new home. You have referred several times during our presentation about your neighbor's home being worth $425,000. But that number represents what they listed it for -- not what someone is willing to pay for it and the proof of the pudding is that while your house has been on the market for the same price for 60 days, their home has been on the market for nearly 90 days and it hasn't sold yet."

That comment hit them between the eyes and I didn't have to say another word. The wife agreed and said that Colorado had always been a dream of theirs and they wanted to kick this into high gear. She confessed that their house had been on the market for two months with only ridiculous offers and if I had not called Ken, they were going to start interviewing Realtors.

If she had not told me, I wouldn't have asked what the highest offer was that she received. She said it was $350,000 and they could not reach their goal with a price that low.

Success tastes so sweet but after we left, Marco reminded me that there were still many steps to take to earn our commission and help fulfill their dream. I also realized that there was a great lesson from Rita's comment. If I hadn't made that call to Ken, and if they hadn't met me, they would have picked up the phone and called someone else. So, no matter how you decide to communicate with potential clients, don't talk about it. Just do it and you will often find a Ken and Rita before Ken and Rita find another Realtor.

CHAPTER 7

Don't Get Comfortable on the Sofa

Marco walked me through all the steps we had to take to list the home. There was staging it to look nice, advising the owners what they should do and making sure they did it. Taking professional photos. Marco used a photographer named Bobbi Smith and 17 years later, I find myself still using her. Once you find a good reliable resource, never let it go. It makes life a lot easier working with someone who you have complete confidence. Sure, I have used other photographers when Bobbie wasn't available, but she has always remained my primary go to photographer. And as with a photographer, you will learn to cultivate a corps of other resourceful and useful support personnel such as inspectors, electricians, plumbers, home cleanup crews, and painters.

We did everything to prepare for the listing and the first open house, which turned out to be a bit of a disappointment because we only had one potential buyer attend. The bad weather certainly played a part in the poor attendance. I expressed my disappointment to Marco regarding the open house, but he assured me that next time would be better, weather permitting. I could not let it bounce off me that quickly until the phone rang. My concern turned from disappointment to elation within minutes of hanging up with Marco. I just received a call from that one person at the open house who said he was going to make a cash offer of $390,000. And on top of it, he was not represented by another Realtor which meant that we would get the entire six percent commission of $23,400 split between the two of us. Less than a month into this business, I had a new love. And remember that saying, "you never forget your first." Nothing could be closer to the truth as this sale started down the path towards closing.

Back on the phone to Marco, I screamed. "The one guy we had today, the guy from the Turks and Cacaos Islands, is going to make a cash offer. He is offering $390,000!"

"That's incredible," Marco exclaimed. "Who is his agent?"

"There was no other agent. He was riding in the neighborhood and saw our sign. He wants his wife to take the kids and come to South Florida so they can go to a good school. He is going to stay in the islands and run his bar and come up to visit every month."

"No agent? Do you realize we are going to get a double on your first contract? You do realize that don't you? Instead of 3% we are getting 6% on $390,000."

"Marco, I'm ahead of you. I've already done the math."

I'm quick with math and calculated almost instantaneously visions of $23,400 dancing to strains of a hot Salsa on the way to our respective bank accounts.

"When do we meet him?" Marco asked.

"Tomorrow afternoon at his apartment."

Wow, what a rush. The first day of making cold calls, I get a listing appointment. First listing appointment, I get the listing. First open house with only one attendee, I get a contract for cash. Everything is going so well what could go wrong. I'm going bananas with excitement. Little did I realize how soon the banana part of the equation would turn to banana pudding.

Our buyer's name was Lucas and there were several ways you could describe him, but the most obvious way was to say he was big. Very big. Lucas stood six foot five at least and would without doubt weigh north of 350 lbs.

I mention this because his size would play a part in how this contract played out. This was an amazing one call, one appointment, one open house, one buyer, one extremely large buyer and several surprises to add to the mix.

The next afternoon, Marco walked me through preparation of the contract and explained how we would guide our new clients through the several documents we needed him to sign. We decided not to tell the sellers yet that we had a contract until we had it signed and ready to present it to them. This was a good practice I cultivated over the years: do not get your client's hopes up until you see the whole picture. At that point you can present it to them. Often you jump the gun and tell them you're getting an offer. If the offer arrives and it's not what you were expecting and you must go back to your clients and ask them to lower their expectations, it can easily make the sparkle fade away.

We met Lucas and his family at 4pm and as we gathered to sit down at the dining room table, he mentioned that he had misplaced his glasses, and would it be okay if Marco read the contract to him.

"Sure," Marco said. "I'll take you through it."

"No, no, please read all of it to me."

Marco looked at me as if to say, this is going to take a while and a while it did. Two hours later with several questions from Lucas to break up the monotony of reading a contract out loud, I was starting to feel hypoglycemic. I have Type II diabetes and had not eaten since noon. The sole banana staring at me in the face in the otherwise barren fruit bowl was starting to call me. Eat me, please eat me. Peel me back and eat me. One hour later, I was desperate and knew if I did not have that banana, I was going to go bananas and faint. So, I finally had to ask.

"Lucas, I haven't eaten since noon, and I am diabetic.

Would it be okay if I helped myself to your banana?"

You could hear a pin drop. Marco stopped reading and Lucas directed a laser-like stare at me as if asking to eat his sole banana had just created an international incident between the US and the Turks and Cacaos Islands.

Finally, the silence was broken when Lucas let a large slow smile melt over his face. His gigantic hands turned towards me, palms up, moving ever closer.

"Mr. Fenster. My banana is your banana," he said with the deepest imitation of a James Earl Jones laugh. "We have more in the kitchen if one is not enough."

Relief pushed out a big sigh as I reached out for the banana. I don't even remember peeling it but sensed that it was immediately providing the nourishment I needed to keep me from passing out right on his dinner table.

Marco started reading again and I detected he was reading about twice as fast, perhaps concerned that I might not make it to the finish line. But within an hour we were finished, and we told Lucas we would present the contract to the Stills the following afternoon and to be prepared for them to submit a counteroffer. Lucas insisted, as was his right to do, that he wanted to be there when we presented the contract. That was the way he did business at home, and he wanted to do it here also. We saw no reason why he could not be there and as we departed; we told him we would call in the morning to confirm a time.

"You bring the contract, I'll bring the bananas," he said with a laugh as he closed the door.

"Marco," I asked. "That went well. Do you often have to read the contract?""In ten years of working in Real Estate, this was the first time I ever had to read an entire contract to a client. Usually, a meeting like this takes no more than an hour but this was long. At least it went well," he replied.

"As a cash deal, how long will this take to sell?" I asked.

"And let's not forget, we only have half a contract. The buyers still must agree to his offer price and that may not be easy. I know they're going to want more, and they will probably want to counter. But if all goes well, we could close a cash offer in two weeks. Let's just take it one step at a time. There's always something that can come up to delay or kill the deal."

"Like what?" I asked.

"The inspection, the appraisal, open permits, liens on the house. You never know until the title company completes their due diligence and you hear the words, "Clear to Close." Fortunately, we don't have a mortgage to be approved so there is no mandate for an appraisal since it is cash, but the buyer can still request one. But assuming we get through this tomorrow it should flow smoothly. I think the motivations of both buyer and seller are strong but let's take it a step at a time."

When we informed the Stills the next morning that their dreams of Colorado and their first Christmas with snow was now on the horizon, they were, to say the least, overjoyed. After weeks on the market as a FSBO with no success, they landed a cash buyer in under two weeks. We explained the buyer wanted to meet them and sign the contract along with them.

"Sure," Ken said, "bring him over. We would love to meet him. Cash you said? Should we have some finger food and drinks prepared?"

We set the time and informed Lucas. If I had been pumped before, I would be sitting on cloud nine now. Just hours away from closing my first deal. And yet, I found a moment to remember what Phil Clodgo said in our class the day before, that the average Realtor earns in their first year $14,000. At that moment I thought I might have picked the wrong profession to ride into my sunset years. But he did say average and when you say average, you must remember that many will be below average and many above and I was going to launch my career above average, way above average. I ran home to my wife delirious with great expectations.

When we all met at the house in the afternoon it quickly became apparent just how alarmingly large Lucas was. Marco and I were men of average height and weight, and the Stills were both short. We were Lilliputians in the shadow of a giant of a man from the Turks and Cacaos Islands. Lucas appeared to be taking up a space equal to the rest of us but when he sat down on the Stills' new black leather sofa, he seemed to melt into it. He even commented that as a large man, it was always difficult for him to find furniture that made him comfortable. He told Mrs. Stills that she had impeccable taste in her choice of furniture and then the negotiations started. Little did I know at the time that the comfortable big black sofa was going to rear up and change the course of our glorious moment in real estate history.

Marco presented Lucas' $390,000 offer. The Stills responded as if Marco had hit them with a brick and then explained why they felt their home was worth more. They were prepared and said they were going to counter at $415,000. Lucas said he would raise his price to $400,000 and the Stills said they would drop to $410,000 but that was it. They weren't prepared to take less even if it was a cash offer.

Lucas stared at them for a long hard moment and finally gave his James Earl Jones laugh that came up from his belly and with a smile said "Okay, $410,000 but I want you to throw in this sofa and love seat. I love it and it's really comfortable."

Mr. Still immediately blurted out that we had a deal but Mrs. Still went into a rant. Oh boy, here it comes, I thought. Mrs. Stills had tipped her hand earlier when we did the listing appointment indicating that she might be tough to deal with and now it was on the table where everybody could see it.

"I'm not throwing in the sofa. We just bought this set and it cost $5,000 and I'm not giving it to you for nothing." Her delivery to say the least was not warm and I could see that Lucas was not receiving it well. Mr. Stills, who felt the deal was reasonable, tried to console and convince his wife that they should accept, but she wasn't buying it. Not at all.

Lucas stood up towering over everyone. In a soft but firm island accent, he said, "I have made my offer. If you choose not to accept it that's fine. There are many more homes on the market, and I am sure someone else will eventually send you a deal. But when I walk through your door, I will not return to negotiate any further. So, catch me on the way out or not at all."

He turned and started to leave. Mrs. Still started ranting again. "Who does he think he is? We paid a lot of money for that sofa and we're taking it to Colorado with us."

Marco and I stood speechless. How could everything be so right and in a nano second, the time it takes to say sofa, be so wrong?

Ken asked if we could step outside for a moment so he could talk to his wife but when he invited us in, he explained he couldn't persuade her that their dream of Colorado was about to be postponed for a while until we found another buyer who would buy the house and leave the sofa.

We did try to get Lucas to change his mind, but he would not. He claimed that he was a man of his word and would not open negotiations to try and make a deal.

The outcome of this quick success and quicker failure was that we were never able to get another offer acceptable to the Stills. They lost their deposit in their

Colorado home and never moved. A few months after the deal died, they asked us to cancel the listing since they had decided they had no choice but to stay in Florida. Perhaps a year later I passed by their house and saw once again a lonely and dirty tilted sign in their yard. For Sale By Owner.

A bit later, I discussed with Marcos if it would have been appropriate to pull the Stills aside and tell them please give him the sofa and we would reduce our commission to make up the difference.

I'm sure Marco also thought about something like that, but everything had unraveled so quickly there was no time. Later we discussed it and regretted not having come to some sort of compromise. But it did enshrine for the future a mantra that to this day I stick to whenever the subject of a prospective buyer wants the seller's furniture. I relay this story to them and emphasize that we are either buying a house or selling it and we are not in the furniture business. After the contract is signed you are free to discuss and inform your clients what you would like to do to dispose of the furniture.

I also enshrined and adopted a saying from Yankee's catcher, Yogi Berra. "The deal ain't over till it's over."

Chapter 8

The Mentor

When your Broker designates the person assigned as a Mentor or Field Trainer, that person will become your guide to all things Real Estate. It is the start of attaining enlightenment in all things Real Estate and it is in his or her footsteps you will find the knowledge to build a successful career. I cannot emphasize this enough.

At the very least, they should make themselves available to shadow you on your efforts to market yourself, to understand and prepare contracts, to prepare and attend your first listing appointments, to help you negotiate deals, to explain the inspection procedures and the appraisal requirements to get to closing. Without their personal guidance chances are you will stumble along the road to closing.

But on a grander scale, they will be your confessor. They will hear your laments when you tell them you think you did something wrong and maybe Real Estate is not for you. They will be your support group to help you get back on track and show you where you made an error and how to correct it.

In most cases they will do all these things because your successes are their successes, and your mistakes can also be their mistakes.

In most cases, Field Trainers have a financial arrangement defined by the Brokerage where they receive a certain portion of the commission of your first few closings. What per cent and how many closings is at the sole discretion of the Broker but the concept is clear.

Normally the more successful Realtors in a Brokerage also take on the task of becoming Field Trainers. It is not a task that can be reduced to an hour a day. They run on time set by a clock with no hands. Whatever time it takes is the amount of time they need to spend with their trainee.

Since they are already a successful Realtor, they probably use much of the information they received from their Field Trainer when they entered the business and if they were fortunate that their Field Trainer always made himself available when help was needed, they understand that they must pay that forward. True, there are Field Trainers who present themselves as accepting the work for the sole purpose of earning more commission and expect to do little to earn it. It will be up to you to determine if your Field Trainer is from that cut of cloth. If you conclude that is the case, ask your Broker to find you another trainer.

However, there is no mandate on the time your Field Trainer will spend with you. If they give you guidance and advice and see that you are not following their lead, they may start to distance themself from you and with repetitive failures to take their advice, they will walk away.

As I said, the Field Trainer receives some compensation from your first few sales but there may be another incentive to want to see you succeed. Many Field Trainers have formed a group or team within their Brokerage. What this means is that he or she has a few Realtors working in a team effort structure. There is a team leader who is the founder of the team and regardless of who makes a sale, the gross commission after the split with the Broker goes to the team and the Team Leader splits that with the team member responsible for the sale. The Team Member's split normally depends on performance and may vary from member to member. It is a simple premise based on the more I earn, the more I earn.

The reason you might join a team after you have made your first sales and feel comfortable on your own is that usually the Team Leader has several years in the business and has developed a marketing plan which provides a brisk business for the team. He or she can then turn much of that business around for team members to handle. The Team Leader splits the gross commission between the Realtor handling the sale and himself.

So, when a Field Trainer observes that a trainee is doing a good job, they might consider recruiting the trainee to join their team and conversely, if they are not performing or following instructions, they will not spend further time with that trainee.

Another benefit of being part of a team is that the preparation of contracts and listings and liaison between lenders, title companies, and condo and HOA associations are usually handled by a team administrator. Sometimes the paper flow and keeping track of critical dates on the road to closing can be overwhelming, especially if you have multiple deals in progress. The team admin relieves you of many of these obligations and allows you to spend more time looking for buyers and sellers and building your business.

And finally, being part of a team allows you to establish a comradery with other team members and provides you with backup when you may not be available. Members of my team have always been available to fill in for a team member who might be on vacation or stuck at home with a bad cold.

For me, building a team provided another opportunity. My youngest son Kevin had just received his degree from Florida International University. While studying at FIU, he also received his Real Estate License.

He was now my partner and he took off at warp speed to immerse himself in the Real Estate industry and success greeted him with open arms. He had the energy that I was starting to lose, and I thought as my partner, the business would continue on past my retirement or that other inevitable thing we cannot escape.

Kevin was building his own future with his sphere of influence and making all the right moves and I could not be prouder as a father and a business partner. But Kevin had other things on his mind. His passion from early childhood was to be a firefighter and he came to me and told me he wanted to qualify as a firefighter. He thought I would be disappointed, but I was not.

"This is your dream," I told him. "It is yours to seek."

I also pointed out as a firefighter he could still pursue his dream and remain an active Realtor. He already had a few good years under his belt and if he stayed in touch with the clients he helped in those first formative years, he would see them return. Plus, firefighters buy and sell homes and with the schedule he kept working one day and being off two days there would be opportunities.

I'm proud of my Hometown Hero and the fine Realtor he has become.

CHAPTER 9

Analyzing the Client's Requirements
Being a Diplomat

Realtors are always analyzing homes for the condition, values, comparable sales in a particular market but they are not analysts in the pure sense of the word. Technically, an analyst is a person who conducts analysis, and the word analyst can be short for psychoanalyst. Analysts guide their patients through counseling and therapy.

But when you listen to a Realtor, the word 'analyze' is sprinkled through every stop on the road to closing. Realtors in a more confined way related to the industry do analyze their buyers and sellers and guide them through a maze of potential obstacles. Often you may feel the persona and comportment of a potential client may need psychoanalysis, but you are not a health care professional, and you need to resist all temptations to provide that type of advice to your clients. As Dragnet's Sergeant Friday used to say, "Just the facts ma'am, just the facts."

Realtors may often be confronted with clients who insist on pushing their personal lives and problems on them. Of course, we set ourselves up for this when we present ourselves as a concerned party and a good listener. Once you open that door, you must be prepared to enter the Twilight Zone which might best be described as ***The Fringe Real Estate Reality Zone.*** But is there really an alternative? I have yet to find one and sometimes you must accept that you are your client's new sympathetic ear. It is more than holding a double-edged sword. It is more like you open the tap to a water faucet and then cannot find the handle to turn it off.

In most cases, Realtors know very little about their clients when they first meet them. And in other cases when Realtors know the client, they find out how little they knew until they start to search for or sell their home. I am not making light of the personal peculiarities of clients who espouse crazy or fringe thoughts. If they give you cause to think they are going to be problematic, that is the time to get off the train. But if you continue with them by signing a listing agreement or buyer's representation agreement, learn from the experience and always remind yourself that you are there to provide services to buy or sell a home.

My first experience with a very strange client came about three years after I was licensed. I had been focusing on getting listings in a particular community in Pembroke Pines, Florida and already had two listings next to each other on the same street.

I took a call from a woman who lived across the street from the two listings, and she wanted to sell her home. She told me she decided to go with me because the two sign posts I had planted in the neighboring homes indicated to her that I was an active Realtor in that area, and she did not want to go with someone who was new to the business or the area. When she mentioned the signs, I flashed back to a day in court a year earlier.

It was a divorce hearing and the attorneys for the husband and wife were arguing before the judge as to who would pick the listing Realtor to sell their house. The wife wanted to go with me and the husband had brought along his choice. We had both brought presentation books to give to the judge to justify our qualifications and marketing plans, but the judge wasn't interested. He had his own method of making the decision.

"I'm not going to rely on the wisdom of King Solomon to make this determination," the judge said with a crisp military cadence. "I've come across this situation numerous times in the past and it seems the cleanest way to go. Whichever of these two Realtors has the most For Sale yard signs planted in front of houses within one mile of the subject home gets the listing."

Luck it was with me. I had two signs and the other Realtor had none, so I was awarded the listing. And now, those big, bright, wonderful, beautiful yard signs were working their magic again.

The selection by my new client and the bonus condo purchase for her husband put me in a great mood but the fact that she was going to pick her soon to be ex-husband's condo made me feel slightly uneasy. Was I being paranoid or perceptive? Still, at that moment this client was going to be easy and the listing was going to be easy to traffic all the way to closing. As I soon discovered, nothing could be more distant from the truth.

I made an appointment to write up the listing and arrived the next afternoon with high expectations. I was fortunate to have one of my new trainees, Pierre Palmieri, accompany me. He was a very bright young man who had resettled from France and spoke English flawlessly. I was going to groom him to join my team. Pierre had been introduced to me by his wife who was a recent client of mine. It is one of the best ways to find talent: people introducing you to other people. Pierre was an excellent recruit and stayed on my team for a few years before deciding to venture out on his own.

When I arrived at her house, she met me at the door along with a man she introduced to me as her soon to be ex-husband. He said nothing to me and just grunted and tried to stay in the background. She explained that if I did an excellent job for her, I would get to buy him a condo. Imagine, they were getting divorced and yet she was still dictating who was going to be his Realtor.

The first part of analyzing the house was the walk through and we were pleased to see that the house was in great condition. It sat on a builders acre lot in a prestigious community.

When it came to setting a sales price, that is when the analysis period started to hit the first bumps. I presented my research to my client recommending a listing price of $550,000.

"That is simply not going to work for me," she said as she revealed a thick multi-binder file that had been resting on a chair under the table and placed it in front of me. "My Analysis of the most recent sales and market conditions suggest that a fair price would be $625,000."

My client had told me that she did not work and was a homemaker and yet she had taken on the role of Real Estate Valuation Expert. Zillow and Trulia accented nearly every sentence from that point on.

I asked if I could review her research and she pulled one sheet from the pile.

"Here is a spread sheet I prepared for you to review."

I had been very thorough researching the most recent comparable sold properties and was secure with my findings that the price should be $550,000. Immediately, I spotted properties that I had passed on because the sale had been over a year prior or that the comparable lot size was three acres whereas her lot size was less than one acre. Others were on lakes with pools and hers had neither. It was very clear that an appraiser was not going to use those comps and that my client had cherry picked the ones which built a case for her price.

I started to explain why her comps would not hold up in an appraisal but felt resistance from the start. And beyond that, I was getting the feeling that she was starting to resist anything I was saying.

When she blurted out that she was sure an appraiser would agree with her meticulously prepared spreadsheet, I immediately felt that my chances of getting the listing were deteriorating if I continued to try and discount her research. If I wanted to be successful, I had to make a mid-course correction. I recalled what a lifelong friend of mine who was a Real Estate developer told me about promoting myself. "Never miss the opportunity to hang your sign." So, I went for the listing and backed off pressing my research. Pierre seemed terribly confused and I could tell he wanted to storm the Bastille and take no prisoners.

Later on, I explained our goal was to get the listing, sell the house, and make a very good commission but there was something else. I wanted to get the third listing on this one street which I knew would lead to more listings. Fortunately, as the story played out, it did just that.

So I stepped back and told my client that I would not have a problem taking the listing at the price she wanted because her house was so beautiful and I was sure that some buyers out there would recognize this. Triumphantly, her attitude of resistance changed, and she smiled I think for the first time we entered her house. Victory was hers. Her spread sheet prevailed.

The cold steel bars that had started to separate us quickly disappeared once I had acquiesced, gritted my teeth and told her what she wanted to hear. I had to remind myself that we were not in a competition, and that I was there to help her sell her home even if I had to take her kicking and screaming all the way to the closing table. She was going to sign the listing agreement. Mission accomplished!

She then asked Pierre and I to wait on her porch for

about fifteen minutes while she took her baby for a walk. She had more questions for me. That struck me as unusual because when we toured the house, I saw none of the telltale signs a baby was in the house unless you counted a small baby carriage which stood out by itself in the bedroom she used for her office. It looked more like a baby carriage from a toy store and not a baby store. The only other life form in addition to her husband who had not even blinked during the whole process was an extremely pathetic looking Terrier that would occasionally yap his way across the kitchen begging, I suppose, for a biscuit.

We moved to the porch and started to fill out the listing agreement as she left for another part of the house. Her soon-to-be former husband had mysteriously disappeared and I returned to filling out the forms until my attention was diverted when I heard the front door open and close. I assumed she had put the baby in the carriage and left the house. But all I heard was the incessant yapping of her dog.

Pierre and I looked at each other with the same questioning look and just two words rolling off our lips, "The dog?"

About 30 seconds later the leather faced husband appeared and sat down in front of me.

"Listen," he said. "We don't have to wait to sell this house to buy me a condo. I want out as quickly as possible and I don't need to sell this house to buy another one. I just want to move fast. Find me a one bedroom in Coral Springs."

Feeling that I understood the domestic situation between him and his soon-to-be ex-wife I suggested, "You might want to consider a two bedroom so that there would be a place for your child during visits.

"What child?" he quickly shot back. He confirmed it.

"Her child is the dog."

Out of the corner of my eye, I saw his wife on the street pushing the baby carriage and pointed to the wife and carriage, "That child." I indicated.

"Ron, did you see a child in this house when you took the tour?"

"No, I just saw a Shih Tzu. Or Terrier or some other dog."

"Yes, that is her baby," he explained.

"And she's walking the baby in the carriage?" I asked.

"Bingo! Cuckoo!," he said with a huge smile finally breaking the crevices of his leather complexion.

The husband was a captain at a Broward County Fire Department. He was tall and although aging, he was extremely muscular yet with every reference to his wife or the dog, he immediately presented a nervous twitch.

"Like I said, find me a condo quick."

On her return to the house, I had to focus on accepting what I had just seen as if it were normal. Two sales were at stake and a slip of the tongue, or a sarcastic smile might sink the entire deal. There was no more analysis necessary.

The end of this listing was a 50/50 score. Pierre sold the husband a condo but we never sold the house and to this day she is still living in it. As time passed, we had numerous listing appointments, but no one stepped forward to offer anywhere near the price she wanted. Each time I approached her to do a price reduction, she would pull her spreadsheets from her file and would remind me that "my spreadsheets don't lie." And of course, she would then blame the failure to sell her home on her Realtors.

I never saw another Realtor's sign on her lawn again but the sign I placed on it when we had the listing did accomplish the mission and the increased presentation of my real estate team landed us another listing across the street.

I am at a loss to offer any advice in a situation like this other than to say make the best of it or give back the listing.

It always amazed me that after nearly 400 listings and sales I still had not seen every type of odd-ball client. Each time I said to myself, "Ron, this last client cannot be topped when it comes to presenting a bizarre pattern of conduct."

There was Martin who lived in a vacation condo/hotel near the ocean. The company that managed the resort owned about 80% of the units and wanted to buy the remaining ones. I was engaged by the owner to buy up the rest of them.

The first few closings went smoothly until I hit Martin. He wanted to sell because, as he explained to me, "My goal is to find a mobile home in the woods away from any child venues due to my son who is getting out of prison for getting into trouble with underaged children."

I decided since he was looking for properties in the Ocala, Florida area I could not effectively help him find his property. Once we were under contract on his condo he wanted to keep extending the date of the closing because he had not found a mobile home to move into. He also kept wanting to renegotiate for more money. In the meantime, I was getting calls from some of his neighbors trying to lobby me to get him out of the condo as soon as possible. It seemed that Martin ran several side businesses at the resort including letting prostitutes use his condo, renting his condo to street people for a nominal sum when it rained so they could get out of the nasty weather, get a hot shower and a clean towel all the while playing loud music at all hours of the night. He was the most hated neighbor I had ever worked with.

Normally, I would have never taken on a client like Martin but in fact he wasn't my client, he was the seller with no representation on the sell side of the deal. My client was the resort owner, and my mission was to buy as many units as I could.

Other odd behavior presents itself in ways that you know from the start that there is no way you should take on a listing yet loyalty to a family member pushes you into it.

I was once doing an open house when a family in the neighborhood came by. They were not interested in buying the house but wanted to talk to me about selling their home just down the street. It was a nice quiet neighborhood and when the open house was finished, I met them at their home to discuss it. It was a modest home that would sell for around $350,000. I kept hard copy listing documents in my car and they signed the listing agreement. The home housed the husband, wife and four children. The only bump in the showing of the home was that with four children, Mom and Dad could not seem to keep the house neat and presentable. Nevertheless, I was happy that this listing fell into my lap so easily.

It took about a month to sell the home and the owners appreciated my efforts so much they asked me to find their new home. Their budget was $650,000. So now between the two homes, I was writing $1,000,000 in business from strangers who just happened to be looking for a Realtor the day I hosted an open house on their block. And it didn't stop there. Once we closed the sale of their home and bought their new home, the wife approached me with a request.

My clients were a great family. The husband was a retired police officer, and the wife was a nurse and also had a school which provided instruction for nurse graduates to take their license exam. The pastor in her church asked her if she would consider being appointed as the guardian for one of his church members who was in declining health and needed someone to handle her affairs during her last days. One of those affairs was the sale of her home. My client accepted the position and reached out to me about the sale of the property.

Once again with a projected sale of this home, the total business provided to me was $1,300,000.

Whereas the first two sales were unremarkable in terms of difficulty, this one presented another problem. The owner who was now spending her remaining days in a hospital had been a successful businesswoman and she had a family I would not wish on anyone. The poor woman was having her home and possessions picked at by her family. They were selling off her clothes and furnishings and trying to get access to her bank accounts and jewelry. On the first day I visited the house, I was shocked that there were about ten people living in this modest two-bedroom home. One of her sisters had rented the house to no less than three families all living under the one roof at one time. Fortunately, my client was able to get a court order to get the families out of the house and we proceeded with the sale. The house was in horrible condition due to the lack of care from the tenants.

I thought that now, my business with this family would end for a while unless they referred me to friends and relatives, but I was wrong. The wife's business was flourishing, and she wanted to find a commercial space for her school.

Within a short time, I found them an office condominium and found myself writing another $300,000 in business bringing the total to $1,600,000 where once again I thought things would grind to a halt.

But COVID hit and her new classroom property quickly transitioned into a virtual on-line school. Her recent acquisition sat dormant while her monthly payments still had to be paid. There was only one thing to do and that was to sell and because she had owned it for only about two years, she might have to sell at a loss, which is exactly what happened. Fortunately, she did not take a large loss and she sold it for what she paid for it but with the closing costs, she was $9,000 in the hole. But the sale now added another $300,000 and I was up to $1,900,000 in business from this family. This surely was the end of the road with them I thought and once again, I was wrong.

They informed me that they had decided to move to South Carolina and asked me to sell the home I had found for them just three years earlier. Prices had skyrocketed and homes matching the size and upgrades of their home were now in the low to mid $800,000 range. When I went to visit them to write the listing agreement, the first thing I noticed was that there was no way their home was going to get anywhere near that price. There were crayon drawings and writing all over the walls. Some walls had holes punched in them. In general, the house was in the same unkempt state as their first home. From all appearances, it looked more like they were camping in the house instead of living in it. They had just put in $50,000 in hurricane impact glass which added to the value of the home but it still needed a top to bottom makeover. I provided constructive advice to have the house painted, the driveway cleaned and sealed and some landscaping suggestions to increase the curb appeal. This family was so nice and if you could create a mold for sellers who cooperate with the Realtors this would be the family to choose. They just had a problem with keeping their home clean. I also told them that the moment the house painting started, take away the kids' crayons.

It took about six weeks to sell the house which sold for $750,000 and allowed them to make up for the loss they incurred on the sale of their office condo. And with this closing my total business zoomed to a final amount of $2,650,000. They were happy with the professional service my son Kevin and I provided for them over the past few years, and I was sad to see them leave Florida for South Carolina.

So, I was surprised that right before they left, they told me that the husband's mother who lived in a 55 plus community had decided to sell her condo and join them in their new South Carolina home.

And this is where the big choice came into play regarding whether to take the listing. Had I not been treated so well by this family and had I not written the amount of business I did, I would not have taken the listing. But I could not turn them down. The mother was a sweet person and wanted to spend her sunset years with her grandchildren but when it came to the sale of her home there were three problems. The first two were real estate problems. The condo she purchased a few years earlier had not managed its reserves well and there were high monthly condo fees and special assessments. Plus, the Condo Association did not allow Realtors to conduct an open house, both items which negatively impacted the sales process. The third problem was similar to her son's house -- cleanliness.

You see, my client was a cat lady. She had two of the largest long-haired cats I have ever seen. She loved her cats and treated them as if they were her babies. They could do no wrong and could take care of their business anywhere they wanted to, which explained why she had multiple litter boxes throughout her house. The entire home smelled like soiled cat litter and to top it off, the cat hair was everywhere. The living, dining room and kitchen had ceiling fans and the hair accumulated on all the blades hanging like Spanish moss on a Florida cypress tree.

Unfortunately, I accepted the listing before I ever saw the home. Although there were several reasons I would have declined the listing or passed it on to another Realtor in my office there was one major reason above all others why I would have turned it down, I am highly allergic to cats!

Aside from now having a listing that required a continuing amount of Zyrtec to service it, I tried to hire two maid service companies who turned it down but finally found a cleaning service company that had a hypoallergenic crew that could clean the condo.

CHAPTER 10

King of the FSBOS

I continued to work with Marco for nearly a year after completing my field training. There was still much to learn. I reached my obligation of splitting the commission on my first two sales rather quickly, but I was not comfortable that filling my obligation was a guarantee of knowing everything I needed to know.

When I decided to step out on my own. I was already getting a reputation in the office that I was the king of the FSBOS, the acronym for properties listed For Sale By Owner.

In retrospect, my first two years in the business were the absolute worst time to become a Realtor due to market conditions enveloped in the turmoil of short sales, foreclosures, fraud and instability. For me, it turned out to be the best because I had to rely on my instincts and to come up with creative ideas to reach my goals and my ideas appeared to be working.

At the time, even without a lot of product knowledge, I attacked my new profession with a never-ending burst of confidence. What was my alternative? My animation project had concluded and with it my additional income. It was a sink or swim moment. I never realized back then that in this foreclosure market you could swim because of your own efforts and through no fault of your own, still sink because of the actions of unscrupulous bankers, brokers, and an endless supply of con men.

With the onslaught of foreclosures and short sales, turning to your fellow Realtor was not always the best avenue for getting advice. It was a period of much confusion and the usual trusted sources for advice did not have the answers. They were as clueless as I was.

Remember when I discussed the necessity of picking the right broker? At this time and in this market, nothing was more important. Small brokerage after small brokerage shuttered their doors. Some were fortunate enough to be absorbed by larger brokerages, but the Realtor market shrunk significantly with Realtor after Realtor leaving the business, not being able to get listings or sales. It was to be certain a time of great concern for the Realty profession. The larger brokerages marshalled their forces and tried to lay out plans to navigate in a volatile market, but it was not going to happen overnight. Banks that were burdened with high percentages of underwater properties had their own issues to deal with if they were to survive. Many Realtors would later recall the feeling of being left out on a limb. Without the knowledge to navigate in an unfamiliar market, they were deeply concerned about their future. But those who did survive this horrible period emerged stronger and more resolute in achieving success than they could have imagined.

Local Real Estate boards and large brokerages like mine jumped in with both feet to create overnight education programs to support the industry in all capacities. Title companies learned how to work with banks and banks learned to work with everyone involved in sales and purchases of distressed properties. But for at least the first year it was not enough. Short sales could take up to a year to process. The shortage of knowledgeable transaction administrators led to the creation of a cottage industry of short sale negotiators and gradually, the industry clawed its way back to a new normal.

During the crash, cash buyers were king. Buyers

needing a mortgage or sellers trying to exit their homes with an upside-down mortgage hit one brick wall after another. Banks were totally unprepared for the onslaught of short sale contracts. It could take days to get someone at the bank on the phone to respond to a question. The county court system had to set up multiple courtrooms where judges would hear foreclosure cases. Intermediary companies professing to be expeditors for short sales were sprouting up everywhere and charging fees which had to be approved by the bank for their services.

You must understand that in a standard real estate transaction paperwork flow is like a ping pong game. You sign something for the buyer, and it bounces to the seller. The seller makes a correction, then it bounces back to the buyer for approval. This can be required for any number of documents and situations and in normal times a 24-hour turnaround to get a document signed by both parties was not unusual. But during the short sale debacle, it could take days or weeks to get a document turned around and the weeks grew into months. During this period, most banks used fax machines and the lines were always busy. Realtors crouched over their fax machine waiting for a response that the fax had been successfully transmitted but the waiting could often require you to bring your own lunch and dinner.

At first, I had no choice but to use either the bank or an intermediary company to try and process the contracts I had written. It was a painstaking process until I started to learn I could create a shortcut by piercing the wall that banks had set up for communication between Realtors and processors. It was never easy but if you applied yourself, you would finally come up with a phone number and an extension that would ring and actually have someone answer. After a while I became quite proficient on my side of document collection, preparation, and submission but as the market continued to crash the banks continued to falter clearing loans so they could close. They were grossly understaffed. Real estate had entered a totally new and unfamiliar arena.

People were panicking to sell their homes and many people were trying to bail out as soon as possible. They tried selling on their own but had no clue how to do it as a short sale. Many 'sell it yourself' homeowners felt they were being forced to enlist the assistance of a Realtor and resented that fact. Many sellers realized too late that when they bought their homes in a surging market, they had been conned into mortgages that were destined to cause them problems down the road with payments which would double and triple. Many of these new homeowners should never have been given a mortgage based on traditional income and credit requirements. But money was flowing from every direction and there was no shortage of takers. New homeowners started to fall behind in their payments and the banks started foreclosure proceedings. When that happened, they tried to sell their homes by any means they could only to find out that they now owed more than their homes were worth. Some felt that real estate professionals were the cause of the crash. It wasn't that they were anti-Realtor. But often the Realtor was the one who sat across the kitchen table and showed them the math which showed that if they sold their homes at the market price, they would still owe the bank the shortfall between the sale price and what the homeowner owed. On top of that, they would have to pay a Realtor commission and that would put them even more in debt. To the homeowner, it sounded like the Realtor who in many cases was the same person got paid to assist them in purchasing the home was now about to profit off their misery. So, they rationalized that if they sold it themselves, they would save the commission and reduce their future indebtedness. They were already past the point of trying to preserve their creditworthiness for the future purchase of a home. Now they just wanted to get out and be obligated for as little as possible. But a homeowner trying to short sell their own home during this market crisis had little possibility of success.

So, early on, that was the market condition I was thrown into and perhaps my ignorance was bliss because when it came to this new brand of a foreclosure market I knew about as much as the more experienced Realtors. No one knew which way the wind would blow, and it was a scary time.

So, I did two things. The first was to immerse myself in every seminar on short sales, foreclosures, and negotiating. Second, I started looking for FSBO's by riding the range in certain neighborhoods that I wanted to sell. I chose neighborhoods with large and more expensive homes where there were no gates or security guards keeping me out. I started a notebook and would record a picture from my car seat of every home that had a For Sale by Owner sign in front of it. I would go back to the office and research the home through the Broward County Property Appraiser's Office and try and come up with some interesting facts I could present at a listing appointment. I had not given much thought to how I was going to get the listing appointment, but I was sure I would find a way.

As it happened, the areas that I picked were Southwest Ranches and Country Club Ranches. These were two communities known for their large acreage properties and horse communities. They were open communities with no restrictions for soliciting homeowners. I found out rather quickly when I started knocking on doors and making phone calls that I was not the first in line to contact the homeowners. Nor was I the 2nd or the 3rd or the 4th in line. I think that I started somewhere around 50th so my greeting was rarely met with warmth and enthusiasm from the selling party. My attempts at the door were met with a cold resistance and I was striking out one after another. I had to come up with a device that would separate me from numbers one through 49.

I had noticed that most of the properties with horses had owners who spoke Spanish. They were from all over Latin America and a few were from Spain. I wondered how these people had ended up here in South Florida and then a question entered my mind. When these people decided to come to South Florida did, they contact their embassies and consulates to find out information about real estate? It was only a thought but maybe there was something to it so I went online to the state department and was able to download a list of every embassy and consular section from every country in the world that had an office in South Florida. I wondered if there was a connection between countries with large agrarian populations, horses, and South Florida. I guess I thought that if there was a connection, people relocating to South Florida who were into horses would ask their countrymen where the best places to live would be where they could have horses. It was a stretch but what the heck.

It's amazing how you can come up with a concept that is so far off the mark and then produces incredible results having nothing to do with the original concept. This was one of those amazing moments.

Everyone in sales has heard of the 30 second elevator pitch where you try to convince someone you want to do business with to buy your product or service during the length of an elevator ride. You know that you have only so many seconds to get your target's attention and make the pitch. It's pretty much the same when you knock on the door of a FSBO home except there is no elevator. Just the threat of the door slamming in your face.

When I would knock on the door or meet an owner in the yard, I would tell him right from the start that I had something to tell them about me. That I was a Realtor. And I was going to show them in 10 seconds why they should use me to sell their home.

Now, I had an eye-catching visual aid. I would hand them a copy of a letter I had composed and the list of every embassy entity that letter went to. Once I did that, I could see by the raise in their eyebrows that they were curious and wanted to hear more. I would then introduce myself and the friendly conversation would start.

I would tell them that the only problem was the letter did not go to the embassy with information about their horse property, but I could easily remedy that if they were interested in selling.

"I can correct that," I would say, and I told them I could sell their home for the best price in the shortest amount of time and I could do it in a way no other Realtor had offered them.

I don't know what to call it but there was some mystique they appeared to like about the approach. Did I get every listing using this approach? Of course not. There were still a few doors to be slammed with my name on it. Nothing will get you 100% of your listing attempts. But I did get a few and most people commented that it was a unique way to expose their home to a market that they had never considered while trying to sell it themselves. I used the unique introduction for a while until the FSBO opportunities receded after 2011.

And here's the kicker. I did send letters to the embassies and consular offices. I recall doing three mailings of about 100 addresses each time. What I do know is that out of those 300 mailings I got one response, but it was not what I had hoped for. The Honduran consulate advised me to stop sending them junk mail. But I did get an awful lot of FSBOS. One FSBO in The Trails of Pembroke Pines I have listed and sold four times since I met the original owner.

CHAPTER 11

Recognizing a Good Idea When It Hits You in the Face

As a new Realtor, you can easily convince yourself that you are going to be able to come up with new original and creative ideas to market yourself. But after a while, you accept the fact that the creation of a new idea is going to be more difficult than you imagined. And implementing it may even be harder. The cost of the implementation is another deterrent and the time it might take, yet another. But don't let any of that stop you. It is part of getting to where you want to be. For me, when I start thinking of a novel idea, I am sure I am on the right track when the idea starts to creep into my dream night after night. The only way I can stop dreaming about it is to set about doing it.

As the history of many professions reveals, many of the best ideas were initiated at the creation of that industry and although time has always made way for improvements, original ideas are much more difficult to spring from an embryonic state. And of course, new, and original ideas that work the way they were intended rise to the list of the most difficult.

I found myself thinking just that: "Where am I going to get original ideas that will set me apart from my competition?" I had already thought about the letters to the embassies and that worked for a while, but I needed something more and something enduring. I started to use traditional concepts in marketing so that I could generate some sort of workflow and create potential buyers and sellers.

In the early days of transitioning to a Realtor, there is no shortage of advice flowing from your broker and other Realtors in your office. Everyone you meet will provide ideas to help you grow your business such as mailings, door hanger cards, telephone calls, subscription lead services. Very few of them will actually slide up close to you as your Uncle Joe might do and say, "Listen kid, I'll tell you what I do to get clients. You just follow my advice, and you'll get rich." It doesn't usually happen that way.

In addition to the people in your office and Uncle Joe, if you are lucky enough to have an Uncle Joe who gives good advice, there is the never-ending solicitation from third party resources who incessantly seek out new Realtors to sell you their sure fire, guaranteed, stupendous product. A typical call was the one I received from a Zillow representative and decided to take the pitch from him. It was an interesting concept where they were dividing up zip codes in blocks of 20% each for a zip code. You could purchase 20%, 40% or the whole zip code. And of course, the more you purchase the more the monthly fee would be. I said why not let me give it a try. It was only going to be $240 a month for 20% of 33029. I signed on the dotted line and got my first lead the very next day. In my book that was impressive. It was from a buyer who was looking in that zip code which was West Pembroke Pines. We had a friendly cordial conversation, and I was excited with the fact that my $240 investment might pay off. As I cemented my bond with the buyer, I thought maybe I should expand the area when another 20% became available and reached out to Zillow. Fortunately, there was another 20% available and I upped my percentage now to 40% of the zip code. The new client was from out of town, and I set up a search on the MLS to send them homes in the area. This went on for about 30 days. They told me they were going to plan a trip to South Florida to view homes shortly and would let me know when.

I thought again that this stuff really worked and called Zillow again to up my area to 60% when it became available. The first month passed with the single lead from the first day. The second month passed with two other contacts, but they turned out to be just window shoppers. In the third month Zillow asked me if I wanted to expand since another 20% had become available. I decided to give it one last shot and increase my area coverage to 60%. I was now paying about $720 a month and not feeling the exuberance I did with the first call. When the fourth month came around, I decided to end the subscription completely. I'd taken a taste of subscription lead services and decided that the $720 a month could be put to better use with direct contact mailings. Regarding the initial lead, they never bought and soon the ability to contact them faded when they no longer answered my phone calls or email.

After I had been a Realtor for about five years I was making a fairly comfortable living but I was well aware that complacency was the gatekeeper of a declining business plan. I needed to make sure that I kept things fresh and stayed relevant to a constantly changing market. I had heard the phrase many times " hiding in plain sight" and on one trip in the field looking for FSBOS, I had that hiding in plain sight moment. It wasn't the fact that a great idea had just hit me in the face, it was more like it had hit me in the rear-view mirror but I recognized there was an opportunity and I set about testing the waters on this new revelation. The fact that I had not heard any other Realtor talking about my new idea gave me more energy to experiment and put it into action.

Becoming the FSBO king of my office required me to log many miles in my car searching neighborhoods for yard signs. Not all FSBOs end up in database files distributed to Realtors by most brokers. So, when I rode the range looking for FSBO opportunities, I also used the time to replenish the flyer boxes that I would attach to the yard signs. Many Realtors shortchange themselves by putting 20 or 30 flyers in a box and think that is sufficient for the month. But the truth is you never know how many people will pass by your property in a single day and how long those signs will last so I always took inventory weekly and carried folders in my car of each property with each folder holding at least 25 additional copies of the property flyer.

One day I was on a street in Southwest Ranches where I had two yard signs each on the opposite side of the same street. I had just finished stuffing one of the boxes and had driven down the street to check the other box. Just as I was about to get out of the car, I noticed someone had pulled up at the first house and was getting out of their car to take a flyer. Instinctively I did a U-turn and headed back there. As I pulled up, I wasn't sure what I was going to say to the person who had just taken the flyer.

"That's my listing in your hands," I told the young man. "Can I help you with any information about the property?"

The words just started to flow easily, and we had a conversation about the property and the area of Southwest Ranches. Before I knew it, we were discussing schools in the area. He asked me about directions to the Army's SouthCom Headquarters and the fireworks ignited. He was active-duty military. I thanked him for his service and told him I had served three tours in Vietnam. In a second, we had bonded, and the tone of our conversation melted into two old buddies having a beer and talking about war and real estate. Of course, without the beer. After about 15 minutes we exchanged contact information with an offer to provide the prospect with other properties in the area.

At this point I still had not defined what the new and novel idea was but as time went by, I asked myself if I could recreate the randomness of this event and meet other potential buyers the same way. So, I decided to test my theory.

I liked selling in the ranches where the community is strung together by small two-lane country roads with very few sidewalks, and plenty of green areas. It's a community that tries to maintain a horse country atmosphere. Most of the streets have areas of shade where you can park your car and sit on the side waiting for something to happen. And that's exactly what I did. I pulled down the street from my signs under a big shade tree, took out a file from my bag and started to catch up on my reading with one eye on the documents and the other on the road down the street. Shortly a car pulled up to my sign and as I placed the file on the seat and put the car in gear, I thought to myself, this might work. As in the first case I pulled up to the car and this time it was a couple who were talking in front of my listing. I introduced myself and again the conversation started with an exchange of information about the house, and then an exchange of contact information.

I was now getting excited that I may have really stumbled across a great idea to meet people who I had personally witnessed were in search of their new home. They were the highest order of what you could call a lead. The only thing I had to do was convince them to use me as their Realtor. But that was not going to be difficult. After all I was already standing in front of them talking about their new home, their budget, their timeline for purchasing and any other subject that would arise. If they had not already found a Realtor, I was confident they would select me. Once in a while, they informed me that they were already working with a Realtor. But occasionally and for whatever reason when that relationship failed to satisfy their needs, they picked up the phone and called me. All types of buyers' leads have a percentage of viability from window shoppers to buyers who need to buy as soon as they locate their dream home. But this type of lead, a buyer standing in front of a home for sale talking directly to me was at the top, a pure 100% qualified buyer.

My mind was swimming with great ideas about this concept. I thought it was just like fishing. No, wait! It was exactly the definition of fishing but with people not dead fish wrapped in newspaper and each one of my yard signs could be a secret fishing hole. All I had to do was sit in front of it and wait for a fish to bite. I loved it.

The initial fishing hole incident occurred purely by accident since I happened to be in the right place at the right time to see someone take a flyer from the box. And that turned out to be a sale down the road. The second time I was not as fortunate. After several mailings of listings, the recipients informed me that they had a Realtor who was a cousin and they had decided to work with him. But that was fine and you will find out that happens over and over again. The concept had worked so I tried it again and again and again. On some days the fish were biting, on other days they weren't, but it didn't discourage me to give up fishing when they didn't bite.

You know when you ask yourself the question what exactly is a 'lead' you realize that it's a potential opportunity. It is not a guarantee. It's information about a person who some database or some lead generation bulletin board identifies as someone who is possibly looking for a home. It is quite different when you see some people getting out of the car in front of a home walking to the flyer box on the yard sign and taking out a flyer and looking at it. That is about as qualified a buyer's lead as you could ever hope for and I thought I had just stumbled on a pot at the end of the rainbow.

Then something else developed from this new idea. The two listings on that street were now sold and my "JUST SOLD" signs were about to be removed from the new owner's lawn. I did not have any more yard signs but as I was driving on the same street, I noticed a car pulling up to a home with a yard sign from another broker. And I thought, "well here's another opportunity." Does it really have to be my sign? Is there anything unethical about stopping to talk with people in front of someone else's listing? After all, I have access on the MLS to that property and can show it to anyone in search of a home so why would this be any different?

I pulled up to that car and introduced myself but this time instead of telling them that the property was my listing I used a slightly different approach and let them know that I was a very active Realtor in this area and had just closed on two other homes down the street. My 'JUST SOLD' signs were still hanging, and I pointed to them for reinforcement. That caught their attention, and we discussed the type of home they were looking for. In this case I was able to help them identify and put an offer in on a home, but the reality was they were not ready to qualify for such a large step up from their current financial position. Nevertheless, the concept now expanded to not only using locations that were my listings but locations anywhere. Two years later, those people called me and told me they were in a much better financial position and wanted to take up where we had left off. I found them their dream home and to this day they are clients getting ready to step up again.

So now I had this great new and novel idea that seemed to be working. And the beauty of it was that it was so simple. You sit in your car. You occupy yourself with reading. Maybe you bring your lunch or catch up on emails, texting clients to stay in touch and suddenly you feel a little jiggle on your line when you see a car swim up the street next to your secret fishing hole. It was just like fishing. No, it was fishing. No, it was better than fishing because you did not have to cut bait or gut your catch and wrap it in newspaper and throw away the fish head.

Now this concept does take patience just as fishing does and just as in fishing, if the fish aren't biting you don't give up the sport. You come back another day and maybe you'll have better results. What I was able to equate was that more listings on the market resulted in more yard signs and more yard signs resulted in more flyer boxes being placed on yard posts and that was the bait. It always amazes me when I see a yard sign without a flyer box. The Realtor who owns that listing for the cost of a flyer box and several sheets of printer paper was shortchanging his ability to sell that house.

During my mentoring sessions with new Realtors, I would tell them this story and how it worked but more importantly I tried to connect with them and explain that qualified leads such as a person standing in the yard in front of a house for sale is the top of the food chain leading to contracts which then of course lead to commissions. And the beautiful part about getting leads from fishing is that you didn't have to pay a cent of your marketing dollars, and you didn't have to subscribe to a service, and you didn't have to give a percentage of your commission away as a referral. And you did not waste your time since you were comfortably working in your car/mobile field office/fishing pier.

I also explained that you had to be very patient for it to work. The fact is that my first catch was strictly luck. But when that one good idea hit me right in the face and came out from hiding in plain sight, I jumped on it.

Remember the quote, "Give a man a fish and he can

eat for a day. Teach him how to fish and he can eat for a lifetime." I just couldn't resist saying that.

But there is a cautionary note to this idea. As I continued my fishing expeditions the market in my farm area started to shift again. More planned communities were sprouting up with gated entries and prohibitions for hanging yard signs. To this day when the opportunity allows, I still go fishing. I attribute the shifting decline in fishing opportunities to two things. The first is that yard signs are becoming, at least in my search areas, fewer and fewer. That could partially be attributed to a sellers' market with low inventory. When homes sell

quickly, yard signs vanish quickly. The other cause could be the Internet and social media where the expanded exposure of real estate is an inescapable part of a home hunter's daily diet.

Driving the roads looking for homes to list or buy is a transition from pre- Internet real estate home searching. But as the Internet and social media expanded, and gas prices increased, driving the roads seemed to decrease.

By no means has this discouraged me, and any time I see a new listing with a yard sign and a flyer box on it, I still find that piece of shade down the street to pull over and keep an eye on the yard sign.

CHAPTER 12

You Bought the Farm, Now What are You Going To Do With It?

"Underneath all, is the Land." Remember that phrase from your licensure studies. I'm not sure if that has anything to do with the use of the word farming to define your geographical area of sales. But let's explore that for a moment.

First of all, you must call your sales area something and a farm is just as good a descriptive phrase as anything else. Over years of use, it has come to include certain concepts of building a market and growing your business. You pick a primary and secondary and maybe even tertiary area of interest to look for leads. That's your farm.

So now that you're a farmer, start farming. The first thing you want to plant are the seeds of thought to create a marketing plan. The plan must have a roadmap to grow your crop and that crop when it blooms will be clients, both the buying crop and the selling crop. And perhaps, a third crop, investments. And a fourth crop, commercial and however many more crops you determine will thrive on your farm.

There is a good visual comparison of how your farm transforms into income just as the labors of a farmer transforms his farm into income. Farmers are very protective of their crops. They try to create an image that makes their crops stand out as a product of the highest quality. You also will become very protective of your farm and you will try to create a great image so other Realtors do not try to enter your fields. You plant the seeds, you water and weed your field and you harvest the results of your labors. Those results are measured in closed sales and dollars in your bank account. And as your farm grows you may choose to expand its size by adding other farmers to your farm crew. And they in turn will add to your success by plowing and planting and harvesting new crops in new fields. And of course, you will own a piece of the crops in the new fields. It's as simple as that.

What you will realize is that the success of your farm will depend on the tools that you use to tend it. In years gone by, those did not include the digital age tools of social media, emails, blogs, and numerous other avenues for exposure. Life in the real estate trenches of that era was certainly more laborious. The road to success was excruciatingly hard and deathly slow. To understand the way business was done and how it affected building your farm, a history lesson helps to appreciate what life as a Realtor was like. Recalling the way business was done back in the day spells out just how hard it was to make a living and makes a point that although today's technology has been an incredible lightning rod at the same time, it has turned many Realtors into the same slow moving creatures of the 50's but for different reasons. Relying so much on technology can make a Realtor become a fish out of water flailing to stay alive when they press a button and it doesn't work. Today, Realtors have their computers, smart phones, and apps. Before the age of technology was introduced into our industry, they had ingenuity, energy, and a never-ending drive to be successful by working hard.

When I was a child growing up in the 1950's on Miami Beach, one of our next-door neighbors became a Realtor. Often at night, the neighbors would gather in our patio and socialize. Air conditioning was just coming into play around this time and not everyone had it. So, sitting outside and trying to catch a breeze was the way neighbors mingled. I can't imagine why I can recall this trivial fact, but I do remember our neighbor telling my parents about the job she got at a brokerage on Lincoln Road. She was excited and said her goal was to become a member of the company's Million Dollar Club which of course meant that she had to sell a million dollars' worth of real estate. Certainly, in today's market that is no great feat but in the 50's it was evidently an important milestone. Information from the U.S, Census shows that the median price of a house in Florida in 1950 was $6,612. If you do the math, it is little wonder selling a million dollars in real estate was a big thing.

The road to success then was measured in how many people you could meet to let them know that you were a Realtor and would love to provide them services. There were very few mass contact outreach avenues at your disposal. Yes, there was still the United States Post Office, but every post card and letter had to be hand addressed. Mass communication was defined as a bus bench. There were community events, civic organizations and private clubs where you could ply your trade but that was it. There was no measure of instant gratification at the speed of a nano second.

If you were working with a new buyer showing houses, your day might have gone something like this. Get to the office as early as possible to search for listings. Finding new listings was not nearly as easy as today where we boot up our computers, enter a password into our MLS and click and scroll a few times to find all the newest listings. Within minutes you can have a list of properties you could show and within a short period of time, you could schedule and confirm appointments and get showing instructions.

Now return to those thrilling days of yesteryear when listings were published usually monthly and could only be found in a large book at your Realty Office. Real Estate

Data Inc., one of the larger listing publishers, had deadlines and if you failed to get your list in on time, it would be another month before anyone might see it. Larger companies might afford a few copies but only one Realtor at a time could search the book. Word of mouth from other Realtors in your office might have steered you to a property or two or you might have passed by a house with a yard sign. So, it required more time to find properties than it would today sitting in front of a computer screen and logging on to your MLS. There was no MLS as we know it today. And when you finally had your list of properties transcribed to your notepad, the adventure in real estate was just beginning.

You then had to call each listing agent and make an appointment and, in many cases, if there was no lock box, you had to go to the listing agent's office and pick up a set of keys with a requirement to return them after the showing. Five homes meant five appointments and possibly five trips to five brokerages. As you can see this was incredibly time-consuming and it would be difficult to handle more than one client in a day. Everything worked more slowly.

How slow? Ask some of the older Realtors in your office how slow. You may not even be aware that the fax machine was a relatively recent invention of the 1970's. It was first referred to as a Phone Dex that had the capability of transporting one single page of information at a time. Not everybody had them in their offices and if you were lucky enough to have one it did not mean your counterpart was using one. And don't even think for a moment that your buyers and sellers owned one. On top of that, it could take you 10 minutes to transfer a contract. So, you had to sit in front of your typewriter or fill the contract out by hand and either put it in the mail or hand deliver it to the listing Realtor. Every time you needed a signature or initial from your client meant a trip to their house or an invite to come by the office. Changes in addendums had to be handled the same way. No one knew that this was an excruciatingly slow process because there was no other option available for comparison. It was business as usual.

Even when personal computers started to populate office desks in the 1990's and fax machines had become God's gift to real estate, there was still a suspicion in the market by many Realtors of the reliability of the new technology and even I who became a Realtor in 2006 remember being asked by Co-Realtors involved in a deal to "put it in the mail." Processing any sort of sale did not come with an option for instant gratification.

Compared to the past, the technology of today has most assuredly spread speed, enlightenment, and opportunity across everyone's desk. Perhaps to a fault. In today's market communications are available to move with such speed that once a contract is sent to a listing Realtor and a response not received within an hour, the sending party is already questioning the listing Realtor's competence, sincerity, or interest.

Along with the increased speed of communication from the desktop to our smartphones came the development of a digital galaxy of applications. Even the word application accelerated and became an 'App.' It just took too darn long to say application. And with the development of the App Age, Brokers started selectively identifying the applications they thought would best suit their minions. It was a period of the cool table in the cafeteria again. Brokerages with great software programs and an unending supply of applications for their Realtors were providing new resources for coordinating how business was done.

The first wave of real estate Apps was an astounding success causing the hunt and peck typewriter to succumb to its long overdue death. Now Realtors had real tools to do fantastic things and as the applications developed and became more user friendly there was no putting the toothpaste back in the tube. Today with AI on our doorstep, applications have moved to the next level which is "why do I have to enter data into anything. I can just talk to my computer screen or cell phone and tell Siri, Alexa, and their cousins to do something for me."

The creation of Apps to keep us cranking out volumes of work product does not appear to have any limits. And yet I for one have become bored with the concept of digital farming. I knew and accepted that it was without question a mandate to the way business is conducted. Call it whatever you want, but the concept itself required you to do things to make your farm grow and you could not do it without your favorite App fertilizer. And of course, using the myriad number of new Apps that would flood the market would continuously make life easier for you. Or would it?

There were programs, web sites, and Apps that your brokerage suggested using. There was incessant texting from people claiming to be your local website builder or lead generator with 100 reasons why you should pay them to use their service. There were water cooler gatherings in your office about which App was the coolest. And let's not forget your real estate board that provided numerous opportunities to help you develop your business.

Now understand I am not a contrarian and just because someone is offering a service, I'm not the type of person who would say you shouldn't use it. What I am saying is that there are so many possibilities to help you grow your farm that you need to walk carefully and assess the ones that you are comfortable with at a price you can afford to pay. And above all ask yourself this question, "Why am I using this App and what is it producing for me?" And perhaps the most important question to ask, "Will using this App separate me from personal contact with my client? If the answer is yes, I would suggest you think twice about using it. But that is just me. I am all in on the direct person to person relationship.

The best example of addressing this last question is computer generated contract with eSigning. Prior to eSigning, a Realtor had to sit face to face with a client for both listing their home and selling it or with a buyer submitting a contract to purchase.

The face-to-face client/Realtor time for listings and sales has entered a pre-extinction era. The time spent bonding with your client demonstrating your competence is disappearing. It has been relegated to an email with the documents to be signed and either a text or phone call to let your client know to check his email inbox. In the long run, I do not think this is a good thing.

It has been my observation that personally reviewing the most important documents in a face-to-face session raises questions from your client. The way you answer those questions is the way you demonstrate your knowledge and competence as a professional realtor.

With eSign programs, you do not even have to tell your client where to sign. The cursor does the work for you.

Even though many clients will still review and ask questions, it is my experience that many do not. Blindly signing docs without a clear understanding of what they are signing is where problems will occur, and I encourage you to take the slower, safer road when it comes to the main documents in a transaction. When an addendum needs to be signed it is easier to use eSign because the addendum is shorter and usually deals with one or two changes which can be discussed on the phone prior to signing.

There is one reason above all others that you should think about when you must decide between the digital domain and the personal contact. Everything I have discussed up to this point focuses on managing a single sale or listing. Going back to the Farm analogy, once you harvest a crop, the field does not die. You churn it and tend to it in such a way that a new crop can grow. And that is the same thing when dealing with people. After your sale closes, how are you going to keep in touch with your clients? Are you going to send them holiday postcards at times during the year or are you going to maintain a closer personal face-to-face relationship? In order to include them and their children and friends high on the list of your legacy clients, I can only suggest that maintaining personal contact with them will work in the long run. A smile, a hug, and a handshake will beat out a computer byte every time.

Most importantly, never forget the sales lessons of earlier generations of Realtors. They didn't have all the digital world has to offer. They had limited resources. They had limited support. And they worked by the standard ticking of a clock and not the speed of a nanosecond. And yet, they sold homes. They earned a living. They supported their families and as time and their reputation marched on, they became better Realtors building a farm that had durability and provided a legacy for those who followed.

Call me an old curmudgeon if you will but as a person who grew up in the fast-paced technical field of film and television and computer graphics, I often long for a slower controlled pace. And during my career, my industry was at the center of the transition from an analog world to a digital world just as the start of my real estate career transitioned the industry from a paper world to a computer world. There are many insecurities in living in any comfortable situation that transitions from a known to an unknown. That does not mean you must be afraid of it or that you have to throw everything aside and embrace it. Just know that at your own speed somewhere down the line you will have to get on board. Like it or not, progress will always break through and shatter old traditions. The secret to applying it successfully is to understand it.

So, I was now at a crossroad trying to determine which way I was going to build my farm. In the office all I heard was, "You must build your farm. What are you doing to build your farm? You need this new App to help you with your farm."

It was a most confusing and perplexing moment of my real estate education. Prior to this time, I was with Marco on his team and I left the farming to him. Now I was out on my own and I had to create a machine that would help me generate new business without me going broke trying every new app or subscription service that came my way.

I decided I was going to create two farms, one for buyers and one for sellers. The seller or listing farm was more easily defined by the question where do I live? I lived in the Enclave in Silver Lakes, a post Hurricane Andrew planned community. We were one of the first homeowners in our development in 1993 and it was now 2007. Many initial buyers had already sold their homes and moved on.

Many new homeowners sell their homes within eight to twelve years of their initial purchase date and the Enclave was a great community to apply that real estate axiom. Having been there for several years my face was familiar to many of the residents. My children and my neighbors' children grew up, went to school, and played together. It would be an initially easy area to work on my listing presentations. That seemed to me a great place to start. I would not appear as an unknown stranger walking up to their door and I thought that my familiarity with many of the other residents of the Enclave would make it easier to engage them in conversations about their current and future real estate needs. But what I found out was other Realtors lived in my community and had started their farms prior to mine. I realized it would take me longer to get listings, but I had to start marketing any way to let people know I was the new Realtor in the neighborhood.

On the buy side within the second year of creating my marketing plan, I was involved in the purchase of a home from a client whose town home I had just sold. The townhouse was in South Dade, and they wanted to move up to Miami Lakes. This was my first opportunity to both sell a house and buy a house for the same client. Little did I know that I was starting out on a venture I refer to as The Gold Rush where I followed a vein of gold until I hit the mother lode. As it turned out, I had the perfect house for them where I was the listing agent. They loved the house, and we made the deal. Then the owner of the Miami Lakes house had me find him a house in Southwest Ranches. That house was also my listing captured as a FSBO. So, within 60 days I had connected the dots between a sale, a buy, a sale, and a buy. But it didn't stop there because both buyer and seller felt that I had served them well and recommended me to two new clients, both relatives, and within six months both those relatives referred me to other buyers and sellers.

Now the dots were connecting at an even greater pace. I felt like a miner who had discovered a small gold vein in South Dade and within a year had traced it to eight other gold veins. Was I on the way to finding the mother lode? And that is when I defined what my farm would become. My farm was going to be a gold mine and I was going to turn in my plow and Farmer John's and get a pair of Levis and a pickaxe.

I created several rules of operation for my mine that today I still live by. It is just like creating an ongoing business enlisting customers as my greatest and strongest crop.

You make lists of the things that you want your company to accomplish, lists for the daily operating procedures, lists of the goals you intend to reach and the lists of the rewards along the way that through your labors hope to obtain.

A lot of people who start small companies are excited with their prospects and create their lists and then place them in a drawer and rarely ever look at them again. I was not going to be one of those people. I was going to set modest but practical goals to achieve and if I did achieve them, I would continue along that same road till I either hit a dead end or found a new road opening up in search of another mother lode.

Dale Carnegie also discussed in his writings the subject of a salesman who is so giddy about making a sale he forgets to ask his client to refer him to others. That is a cardinal sin for the salesperson in any business. Don't be that salesperson. Don't wait till tomorrow. At the closing when everyone is happiest ask for that referral.

CHAPTER 13

The Right Person for the Right Job

It is almost inevitable that when you form a team you will have Realtors join and within a year or two even if they are successful, they will exit the team to seek greener pastures. The math does show that if they continue to get listings and sell homes, they will make more on their own. Some Realtors are comfortable being part of a group that allows them to grow with the group and others for whatever reasons might want their own team. The advantage of finding a comfortable position on a team is that the team leader is normally responsible for many of the costs of marketing and overhead that the team might incur. It is not unusual when starting your own team that your personal workload increases because you now have other functions to handle that you didn't before.

Almost all my trainees were able to move on and produce good revenues for themselves. There were some, however, who never really caught on even while they were on the team and were always more concerned with their commission split.

When I am in a training session and recount some of my experiences in the field, I never pushed my trainees to accept doing things my way. I am not a 'My way or the highway' mentor. I try to provide enough information and guidance to let each trainee find their own comfort level. I would tell them of a situation I had during a listing or a sale and let them absorb the story. What they could draw on for future use in their sales or listing appointments was up to them. After all, I was not their boss: I was their trainer.

As I said earlier, war stories in my opinion are the best way of absorbing information about doing real estate deals. You really can learn from the successes and the mistakes of others. And it is especially the mistakes that I made which I shared with my trainees to try and keep them from falling into the same situation.

In 2021 I had the opportunity to welcome aboard my team a former trainee named Jill. She was an extremely pleasant person with a great sense of humor and the desire to learn everything she could and make a lot of money. Jill was a single mom with a full-time schedule dedicated to her teenage daughter. That ate up numerous hours every day. But Jill was organized and whatever time necessary for her real estate, she would spend applying the lessons she learned during our training, field sessions and open houses. So, with her daughter, Real Estate, and an engraving side business she was developing, her plate was as full as a single mom could handle.

In addition to the time spent with me, she immersed herself in numerous training courses, webinars, and online lectures. I never had to push her to do it. If she found the subject was going to provide her with more tools to success, she would make the time.

Jill also developed a skill outside of real estate that she currently applies to keeping her name in front of her clients. Before she became a Realtor, she bought a laser engraving machine which allowed her to produce a myriad of different crafts that could all be personally engraved such as mugs, glasses, and cutting boards. She honed her skills with each successive order and was able to customize her art on nearly any type of material. With each sale, Jill handcrafted a beautiful gift for her client, and it was the useful type of gift that a client would use and thereby remember her.

I want to talk about Jill because she epitomized the perfect model of how a new Realtor should manage their time for family and work. She had no reservations about rolling up her sleeves and balancing her time at home, in the office and going into the field to work.

Jill lived in a planned community of a few hundred homes. She had lived there for several years and so was already known to many. From all the tools I showed her that were available to farm her community, she chose mailings, door knocking, and networking. The first year of farming her neighborhood she captured four listings. It was an unqualified success, but it was only a success because Jill was not afraid to get out on her farm versus sitting in the office in front of a computer screen hoping some cyberspace revelation would land in front of her and provide listings.

I was also able to help Jill with potential buyers by letting her help me with my open houses. The deal was simple. If the home was sold, I kept the listing side of the commission on the sale. But if a home buyer came into the house and was not represented by a Realtor, she would get the majority of the Buyer commission. She would also have the opportunity if a buyer did not buy the house, to enlist that buyer as her client and show them other homes. As I have mentioned, an open house is the quickest way for a new Realtor to find buyers. During the many open houses Jill helped me with, I was able to listen in on her presentation and offer suggestions for improvement. The training wheels came off rather quickly and soon she was flying through a home rattling off facts about the home and community as if she had been doing it for a dozen years.

When Jill captured her first listing, I impressed upon

her the importance of conducting an open house. Many Realtors detest open houses.

"They don't work. Only nosey neighbors come." you will hear time and time again from the naysayers. Jill knew better having participated in several already. She knew if applied correctly they work better than you could possibly imagine.

Conducting an open house has many benefits. In addition to trying to find a buyer for the home, you are going to meet people who are not represented by other Realtors. This of course means you are possibly going to get a double paycheck when you sell the home. But it goes beyond that. If you have a good open house with 10 people, you are probably going to walk away with a couple not represented by another Realtor. This is where you step in and convince the buyer to use you to search for their new home. There is nothing theoretical about this process. One of Jill's clients she captured was a couple from New York. She impressed them at the open house and eventually made a $925,000 sale at 2.5%. So, spending a few hours on a Sunday afternoon, she racked up a gross commission of $23,125. By any stretch of the imagination, that was an afternoon well spent.

But wait, there is more! The beauty of conducting an open house is that it doesn't have to be your listing. Remember those Realtors I said hate to do open houses? You will find them in your office. Seek them out and ask them if you can conduct an open house on their property listing. They will still get the sale if someone puts in a contract but if that buyer is not represented by a Realtor you are going to get the buy side of the deal. And in addition to receiving the buyer side commission, you can still end up with additional potential clients. Those other buyers who walked into the house and did not buy it gave you an opportunity to find them a new home. It is the most incredible winning situation that you could possibly have. And in my opinion, an open house opportunity is a gift that can keep on giving.

One other tip to remember is to always have your computer and Wi-Fi available. Sometimes you will get a potential client who comes in and is so engaging that you want to show them houses online right away. So be prepared to have all the tools you need to capture your new client.

Some Realtors can go overboard with open houses. They buy a lot of food and bring in a lot of drinks and wine thinking that they're going to have 50 people show up. It doesn't work that way. In an active market on a good day if you get 10 to 12 people that's great. But if it rains on that same day, you may get none.

Brokers open houses are different. When a Broker holds an open house, the attendees are other Realtors. They are usually held at lunchtime or after work and the broker presenting the open house uses food and beverages as a lure to get Realtors to attend. But with a regular public open house you don't have to really go out of your way. If it's a hot day, having cold drinks is certainly a benefit but to produce a whole lunch for an undetermined number of people is not in my opinion the way to go. And it will sour you on future open houses if you spend a lot of money on food and very few people show up.

So, with Jill, I showed her how to do her first open house and for a while, it nearly ruined her concept of what an open house should be. The market was soaring, and inventory was dropping. As prices started to rise, available homes were flying off the MLS as quickly as you could list them. It was shortly before COVID ravaged the country. South Florida was starting to see a mass migration from Northern states.

Jill had gotten her first listing in her community from walking the neighborhood. She came across a man cleaning out his garage. It was a nice two-story home on a lake with a three-car garage and a pool. It sounded like the ideal listing but was as far from that as you could possibly imagine. The owner had passed away and regrettably during the last years of his life he became a hoarder. His garage was crammed from floor to ceiling with all kinds of memorabilia and junk. Jill had met the son who lived in Chicago and oversaw settling his father's estate and selling the home. Jill's effervescent personality allowed her to bond well with the son and to come up with a game plan to clear the house of everything that the son did not want to keep. Some people might consider this a chance happening or just plain luck that she met the son at the precise moment she was walking the neighborhood. I would suggest otherwise. It was not luck, because Jill was in the field practicing what Realtors should be doing. If she had not decided to capture and aggressively build her farm, the son could easily have been met by one of several other Realtors who lived in the community. Later, we learned that the next-door neighbor was looking for a house in the community for their daughter. It was almost inevitable that the neighbor would have encountered the son if Jill had not arrived first. There are just certain things that you cannot accomplish sitting behind your desk. Walking the fields on your farm is one of them.

There was a lot that had to be done before we could put the house on the market. We had to paint the house, do kitchen and roof repairs, and replace the carpet. During the owner's final years, he also failed to maintain the home. Once we got the home in shape, we listed it and scheduled the open house.

This was Jill's first open house and one of the prime bits of advice we discussed when we talked about staging was not to be cheap on the open house signs. So many times, when I would attend an open house, I took note that the listing Realtor only had two or three signs out. The sign in front of the house often had balloons on it. Every home usually has multiple roads entering the community. You want to make sure every single one of those roads has a sign on it or you are doing yourself a disservice. Imagine if a house has five ways to approach it and you have only placed two signs on two roads. That is only 40% of the visual opportunity to see this home. And 60% will not see your beautiful balloons.

On that day Jill arrived early to set up. We checked the weather, and it was going to be hot so we made sure we had plenty of water. People were also starting to wear masks, so we decided to allow two couples at a time in the house. We had already seen traffic at other open houses starting to soar to a point where twelve buyers would be considered a bad day. So, we were very anxious to see how things would go.

As I pulled into Jill's neighborhood and approached the house, I could already see cars parked bumper to bumper on both sides of the street and when I rounded the corner to view the house, there was a line of at least 40 people outside the door. As soon as I could find a parking space, I ran to the house to help Jill. She was only letting two couples in at a time and letting them roam freely with brochures on the table that they could pick up. All the other people were standing in a ragged line outside and around the corner waiting to get in while trying to keep cool in the sweltering Florida sun.

"Where did all these people come from," I asked her.

Carrying several small bottles of cold water towards the door to hand out to the people outside she said, "I guess I promoted the house too much."

"No such thing. You can never promote too much," I shot back as I grabbed more bottles of water and followed her out the door.

It was the best open house I had ever been involved

with and it just didn't happen on its own accord. It came from good planning and good promotion, part of which was to walk the entire community the night before and let every homeowner know that we were doing an open house.

Many homeowners would like the opportunity for friends or relatives to live near them and letting them know that there is a home available in their community can assist in the sale of the home. I do recall that with this particular property, we had a prospect adjacent to the home and one across the street who put offers on it for relatives of theirs. Neither of them was granted the contract because their prices were too low but the concept of exposing the home to the existing community enhanced the exposure.

Jill was able to expand the success of her first open house in this neighborhood and within the year had acquired additional listings and additional clients. She was now threading the golden vein looking for the mother lode.

CHAPTER 14

You Are the Fly on the Wall

As a residential realtor you are invited into people's homes and like it or not, you will be exposed to moments that may put you in an uncomfortable position. Although most sellers act in an appropriate manner, there are others who tend to spew out facts about their lives, their relationship with their spouse who is on the deed, their children, their medical conditions, their politics and on and on. All you want to do is get the listing and sell the house. Although they seem to want to engage you in their problems, you try to avoid setting yourself up to become their resident counselor or psychiatrist. Yet every chance they get, they want to lean on your shoulder. It is difficult to stop them from providing you with information that has little or nothing to do with the sale of the house. You can stand tall and tell them you do not want to get involved in their personal lives, but you do so at the risk of offending them and losing the listing or the sale.

Sometimes the situation deteriorates from uncomfortable to disturbing for other reasons. That can be from the way the house is maintained. Does it smell? Do they have pets and don't clean up? Do you notice things about children living in the house that concern you?. It is not easy to turn a blind eye.

I'm going to lay out six situations that I personally experienced. It is not my intention to present these situations in a humorous tone. You may laugh at the descriptions, but the seriousness of the events cannot be understated.

Sometimes it might be difficult to accept the situation you walked into, and you want to know how to get out of it. When you describe to someone else what you just experienced, it often comes out in a humorous way because it is so crazy that laughter is the response. And often it ends with the person you are talking to saying, "I wish I could have been a fly on the wall to see how you got out of that predicament."

HOARDERS

People who have large amounts of collectibles and memorabilia scattered throughout their house or kitchen counters packed from the backsplash to the front of the counter or bedroom closets crammed with clothes are not hoarders. Nor are homeowners with garages stuffed with so much that a car can't fit in it. Nor are people who collect every miniature hotel bathroom shampoo, bar soap and shower cap. These homeowners just live in a cluttered environment.

The difference between these people and hoarders will be immediately noticeable when you enter a true hoarder's house. What makes it so obvious? In most cases you will not be able to easily enter the house. The front door will not open completely due to clutter on the inside. No matter how much you push forward it will not fully open. For entry you might have to enter through the garage which also will be packed floor to ceiling with everything you could imagine and much that you could never imagine.

The first thing that comes to mind when you enter a hoarder's house is how on earth am I ever going to sell this? Let me tell you that from my experience it won't be easy. When you explain that everything must be taken out of the house you hit a wall. The blank expression and the quizzical look from the owner will hit you right between the eyes. I immediately offended one hoarder even though I was careful not to refer to his possessions as junk when I referred to the collection items as 'unattractive stuff.'

He snapped at me, "Listen here, this unattractive stuff as you call it is important to me and it is going to my new house."

Once I encountered a hoarder who initially was still alive and living in the house. Shortly later, the hoarder had passed away and I was dealing with a member of the estate who assessed the situation as problematic and instructed me to find a way to clear the house of everything but family memorabilia. That was considerably easier because there are companies you can call to empty the contents of a home.

One time several guns were discovered in the house, and we called the police to pick them up. Another time we discovered urns of ashes of loved ones and had no idea what to do with the deceased because the surviving relative did not want them. In the worst-case experience, the living room was packed from floor to ceiling and when we finally emptied it there was a piano sitting in the middle of the room. On top of the piano, there were dozens and dozens of new items of clothing that had never been worn and were just piled to the ceiling. Hoarders do not just pick up junk to take home; they spend vast amounts of money on new things and never use them.

Other items you will find are just plain junk. They have absolutely no use other than in the owner's mind. There's a cable show on one of the networks that tells the stories of hoarders, but I've never seen anything as bad as the one house that I've described. It took three large trucks to empty the place. The deceased owner had packed her house to such a degree that in her final days, she slept on a mattress on the floor in a guest house outside by the pool. And even that was difficult to enter.

Another time I dealt with a hoarder who was still living in the house and the situation required working with a court appointed caretaker. The court finally gave the caretaker power of attorney to list and sell the house once the owner had been transferred to an assisted living facility. Then the unexpected happened. The court appointed caretaker was pounced on by relatives and people claiming to be relatives trying to get hold of the owner's money and valuables. This person had been a successful home health care provider. When her health deteriorated, she had to be placed in assisted living. She had money in the bank, fine clothing, and jewelry. When I went to the house, a sister of hers had already moved into it and was renting space to strangers. It was a very bizarre situation and something that was above my pay grade to manage. I had to press the caretaker to go to court and get the authority to evict all these people otherwise we would never have been able to get the house in shape and sell it.

You might think it's easy to just separate yourself from the trauma of a situation like this to just the real estate portion of this person's life but in fact it is not. And the only way I can suggest handling something like this is first to discuss it with your broker who might have prior experience in such cases and have suggestions for you to follow. Keep in mind that you are still dealing with a living person and have become, for a time, the caretaker of their property. Your client is a person who once lived in that house and probably raised a family with laughter and tears that came and went through the years.

BIGOTS

Bigots come in all shapes and sizes. And their bigotry spreads across many prejudices. When you are convinced that you are in the presence of a bigot in my opinion the best thing is to walk away. But sometimes bigotry does not raise its ugly head until you're so far down the road that it is difficult for you to extricate yourself.

In our studies to receive our license, we learned about situations where prejudice lives. For example, redlining was once a fairly general practice to define the racial and ethnic makeup of a geographical area and to either keep people from moving in or moving out. In any case that's a practice that's more easily recognized. But what happens when you're sitting in the listing appointment and someone says to you, "I want to make sure that you don't sell my home to any Jews or Blacks. I'm using the words 'Jews and Blacks' but those were not the actual words that were presented to me.

On one occasion while training with Marco Zarfati, we were at a listing appointment in SW Ranches, a horse community in South Florida. I had just secured a four-acre FSBO listing across the street. I got the appointment by calling a FSBO sign in the owner's yard. This other listing was also a FSBO but I had a hard time connecting with the owner. I was able to enlist the owner of the first listing to open the door to his neighbor. The owner of the first listing warned me that his neighbor was a "bit off his rocker." While Marco and I tried to move forward on our listing presentation, the owner of the house kept drifting into politics. We would get him back on track and he would drift off on another subject having nothing to do with selling his house. Finally, he went off on a rant blaming Jews for the current real estate market and for the economic woes of the world. Marco and I were both

Jewish and looked at each other with the same message. We both turned from the man and left his house. We didn't even say goodbye. For several years, I would pass this house and the FSBO signs were still hung on the coral stone wall.

A few years later during a listing appointment I had my second incident. The owner of the house was taking me on a tour when we entered a room that had WWII pictures hung from floor to ceiling on every wall. The pictures were of German armed forces and death camps, interspersed with the photos was Nazi memorabilia.

"Pretty cool stuff," he said as he leaned into me with a smile.

"I don't think so," I shot back and told the owner that I was not willing to work with him and just walked out of the house.

But other times you are so far down the road that you must come up with an alternative response or if necessary, walk away.

In another case. Jill and I had sold a condo in a 55+ community owned by a 57-year-old man. His mother was a retired nurse and was on the deed of the condo we were selling. The son was going to have a problem getting a mortgage due to his low income, so his mother was going to have to assist. At our first meeting, he told us he had to sell the apartment because it was noisy at night and he kept hearing people talking and could not sleep. Additionally, he maintained his unit had a roach infestation problem.

"There are roaches everywhere," he would often remind us.

We were in the apartment dozens of times, but I never saw a roach. And coupled with his complaint about hearing voices at night, Jill and I were thinking perhaps there was an imaginary issue specific to our client.

His mother was legally blind and already had the

burden of taking care of another son who had mental issues and lived at home. She was, to say at the least, a very annoying person but manageable. I had been in the business long enough to accept the fact that you must work with all types of personalities with all types of issues, so that was no reason to walk away from the deal.

The sale of the existing property was challenging but we successfully sold it fairly quickly. It was a first-floor unit and in 55 plus communities first floor units are in demand.

During the closing period of the sale, we were also focused on trying to find our client his new home. Every property that we presented was like a wrestling tag team fight. If he liked it, she hated it and if she liked it, he hated it. An excessive amount of time was spent showing them homes. Finally, we found a 55 plus community where they were both on the same page. Then the deal hit a roadblock when it became clear the association board did not want to approve the son. Until that point, we were completely unaware that our client had a prior criminal record soliciting for prostitution. Nothing violent, but enough to create a problem for his approval.

Out of the blue, the mother called us and started ranting about how we were not doing a good job representing her son. She was not being clear and I asked her to be specific about her complaints.

"The Board is full of Jews, and they do not like Puerto Ricans," she said.

We told her we would investigate the reason her son was being denied and get back to her.

That hit Jill and I directly between the eyes and Jill, who is not Jewish, suggested we walk. I agreed. Out of curiosity, we checked the names on the board of directors to see where this woman would get such an idea. There were a few Jewish sounding names, but the majority were Anglo and Hispanic.

OFF THEIR MEDS

So, what do you do after you sign a listing and start representing a seller and their personality takes a violent 180-degree Dr. Jekyll and Mr. Hyde swing?

I had a client in my own community who contacted me to sell her house. It was a small three-bedroom two bath first floor condo and with inventory being low, I thought it would be a reasonably quick sale. I had met the seller a few times in the community, and she was always pleasant. When we signed the listing agreement and took the photographs, she was the sweetest person you could possibly imagine. However, the one thing she was not was a good housekeeper and her house, to say the least, was filthy. When I touched her granite countertops, my hand would stick to them from the accumulated dirt and grime. Her floors were filthy, and her bathrooms needed major cleaning. Yet when I brought the subject up to let her know that we had to get the house in shape and give it a good cleaning, she took it in stride and said she would take care of it. It did not seem to offend her, and I could not imagine that her mood was about to take a quick turn.

What was also odd was how sparsely the house was furnished. Both of her girls had a bed and small dresser in their room. Additionally, there was a table with gaming computers. The living room did not have any furniture. At one point I asked her if she had shipped a lot of her goods to her new home. She just shook her head and told me that everything in the house was everything they had. It seemed that they were camping in the house and not living in it.

On the second weekend after we got the listing, I held an open house. She had already left with her two daughters. A couple had just entered the home and I was starting to show them around when my phone rang, and it was her. Before I could even place my ear to the phone, I heard her screaming that I had not closed the door tight, and dirt would blow in. The couple I was with could hear her screaming. I gave them an uncomfortable look as I quickly looked over my shoulder and saw that the door was closed so I did not understand what she was complaining about, but I was more concerned about the ferociousness of her verbal assault. I was not going to argue with her in front of the two potential buyers and I told her that I would make sure that the door was closed and would get back to her as soon as the current viewers had left.

As soon as they did leave, I dialed my client and asked her why she was screaming at me since the door was closed. She started screaming again to stop lying to her and I should know she was parked across the street watching me. I asked her why she was watching me and she said that "She knew about people like me and wanted to make sure that the people attending the open house did not leave with anything."

"What does that mean?" I asked.

Raising her voice again she said, "I know what you are doing!"

I asked her what that might be, and she hung up. Now this is where you start to ask, "Is this person off her meds?" Well, that was not for me to decide because I didn't know if in fact she was on medication. And of course, I am not her physician and really it is none of my business. When you find yourself in a situation like this, it can become more uncomfortable as time goes on and I felt I should share the incident with my Broker and see what she could suggest to put things on track.

The relationship between this client and me quickly repaired itself and she was the sweet lady that I had first met and then it disintegrated again from day to day, and kept ping ponging back and forth.

Then she started calling my Broker to complain about me. Fortunately, we were able to get into a contract before the relationship was permanently fractured. But even on the road to closing, she would call my Broker to complain.

After the first barrage of screaming, I put the situation before my broker, Bonnie Josefski. Bonnie and I had worked in the same office for several years before she became the office broker-manager. She is an energy propelled woman with a contagious laugh and a get things done attitude. And she always makes time to try and head off problems before they get out of hand. She was not surprised by my description, having received the first of many calls from this client complaining about me.

I had always made it a practice with prior office brokers to immediately put forth any situation I thought might see getting out of hand. I thought it would always be better if they had some information about a situation before the phone rang. Also, there was nothing to guarantee that a complaint would go to our individual office broker. The complaining party could try and go directly to corporate headquarters and right to the President. Office brokers do not like to be caught off guard, so my advice is always keep them in the loop if things are getting tough in the trenches.

We closed on the deal and never really understood the source or reason for my client's never ending ping pong of personalities. But, like the saying goes, just go with the flow and get to closing.

HE DIED BUT THE DOGS DID NOT GO HUNGRY

I received an unsolicited call one day from a

gentleman in Jacksonville, Florida. He told me he was a nurse and had a lifelong friend who was a doctor that had just passed away in South Florida. He got my name from another nurse that I helped find a home.

He said that I had a great recommendation and that he wanted me to list his deceased friend's house. I asked him if he was going to be down in South Florida so we could sit down and discuss the listing and marketing and he was very direct and told me he had just returned home and to just research what I thought it was worth and he would go with my recommendations. I asked him to send me his power of attorney and he said he would do that right away.

So, I thought this was going to be easy and to top it off, the house was in the development right next to my house on a big lake in the Silver Lakes Community. I did my research and sent him my recommendations and then followed it up with a call. He said my recommendation was acceptable and to send the documentation and he would sign it and we could get started. He also said he would send me a key to the house overnight. I had an inkling that this was going too smoothly and could turn into one of *those* situations. Of course, you can guess the answer. It certainly did.

When I was just about ready to thank him and hang up he said," There are a few things more I need to tell you about the house and the deceased."

"Okay, I'm listening," I told him while I thought, Here it comes.

"The house is beautiful or I should say it was beautiful. It sits on a lake with a pool surrounded by lots of lush green trees. It has a three-car garage and sits on a large cul de sac. My friend lived in the house by himself with his three Great Danes." He went on, "He died in his sleep, and no one was aware of it until five days later. He had a girlfriend who lived in Hialeah and after the third day of not being able to contact him she thought that something might have been wrong. On the 5th day she was able to enter the house."

With the mention of the three Great Danes, I could see where this was starting to go.

He continued," Ron, right before he passed, he bought several large bags of dog food and after the dogs started getting hungry and had not been fed they broke into the bags to feed themselves. Understand that these are large dogs and for five days with my dead friend in his bedroom they feasted on all the bags of dog food. There was a monthly supply. I don't know if you can imagine what kind of a mess that made. But please don't worry, I had already gone down to the house and was able to get the dogs into a temporary kennel and get all their droppings picked up. What I was not able to do was get the smell out of the house. I don't know how we're going to do that, so I'll need your help."

Well, here is a new line of work for me: founding partner in Ron Fenster's Real Estate and Hazmat Cleanup company.

I could almost feel myself gagging at the thought of entering the house. But I told him there were companies that could go in and restore it in a manner that would allow us to put it on the market. Even as a pet owner, my estimation of how bad the house smelled was way lower than reality.

The next day I entered the house and as quick as I entered, I had to run out. The dogs had done their damage on beautiful Persian rugs and the scent was embedded with a vengeance. He had been right. The house was beautiful at one time but no one would notice that unless we were able to sanitize it.

Evidently situations like this happen more often than one might think, and it has spurred the creation of several businesses which deal with this type of house cleaning. I interviewed a few companies and recommended them to my client.

After the sanitation process, we hired a painter to completely paint the house so that residual odors could be eliminated. I arranged to have an open house and get rid of the deceased's personal property that was left in the house and then put it on the market.

It also turned out that the owner was a gun collector and had nearly 100 guns in the house with boxes and boxes of ammunition. It seemed between the three Great Danes and the Guns he was preparing for Armageddon. I was able to dispose of the guns and ammo also.

I had asked myself if this was part of a Realtor's responsibility. To sanitize a home, get it painted, get rid of furniture and guns? No, it's not, but if you want to sell the house, it is.

CAN YOU PLEASE MAKE A DECISION?

There are many people who have difficulty making decisions. Once again it is not our job as Realtors to psychoanalyze them and get to the bottom of their decision making capabilities. And usually in my experience their ability to make a decision can be evident right from the listing appointment. If you listen carefully to their comments, you will notice a tendency to agree and then disagree.

I was contacted by a seller referred to me by a neighbor. He wanted me to list his house and set up a meeting to discuss it. I did my research and kept the appointment we had set for the next day. As I went through my market analysis and presented my recommendations, he sat silent.

And then he said," That all sounds good, let's do it."

We signed the listing agreement, and I made an

appointment for the photography and concluded the meeting. The next morning, he asked if we could have another in-person meeting and I responded, "Sure, why not." I had no idea what he wanted to discuss.

When I arrived at his house it was as if we had never met the night before. He asked me to review my research, so I asked him if there was something I did not cover the prior evening. He said no, he just wanted to review everything and make sure he was okay with it. I thought that was fine and I spent some time reviewing my market analysis again and then he asked if I could go through the listing agreement again and I agreed.

There was a lot of work to be done in the house. He had raised his family there and his wife had passed away about six months earlier. He was planning on retiring upstate near Ocala, Florida. When I finished reviewing the listing agreement and answering his questions, we discussed building a road map of what we had to do to get his house on the market and get to closing. He was concerned that he would not have time to clear out his home because there were 30 years of memories in it. I discussed the current market situation with him and said that he was in a good position to sell but that we should not wait too long to get it done because the market had been on an increasing rise for several years and could be due for a pullback. He asked if I could put the listing aside for a month to give him some time to try and get his house in order and start packing things up. I told him that would be fine, and we agreed to meet again in another month.

When the month had passed, I called him again and he said he was ready to execute the road map. I went to his house to update the listing agreement and eyeball the progress he had made clearing the place out. We made some changes to the listing, and I returned to my office to start inputting the listing when the phone rang. It was him again. He said he thought that he might need another month. Now, I was starting to see a pattern.

I asked him if there was a problem in getting the house ready and he said it was just difficult for him to decide what to keep and take with him and what to give away or throw out. He did say that he had arranged many items in groups but had not even packed one box.

Nearly a year later we were finally able to put the listing on the MLS and the packing had barely taken place. I thought that if we got a sale, that might motivate him to start packing. But I made sure once we went under contract that the buyer gave us at least 90 days to exit the home because I knew this was going to be a problem.

The purpose of this story is that again you're dealing with people who may have issues that are not your issues but for you to consummate a deal you have to find a way to work with them. In this case, I was eventually able to meet the children and enlist their aid trying to get the father to make necessary decisions. It did not go as quickly as I would have liked but I did not see any other choice but to march to the beat of his drum if I wanted to make the sale.

ARE BUYERS REALLY LIARS?

One of the first expressions you will hear from your colleagues when you start your career is, "Buyers are liars." When you ask them to explain, they will tell you a whole litany of things such as, "They said they were pre-qualified but they were not. Or their credit score wasn't close to what they said it was. Or when I asked them if they could afford to buy their new home without selling their old one, they said they could but in the end they could not." These are only a few of the comments and I have personally heard every one of them.

When a client provides information that shortly turns out to be incorrect, it is irritating to the Realtor because they may have already spent a great deal of time working with the client. Then they suddenly find out that they cannot qualify for a home and all the time you invested is down the drain because the client lied. Sometimes it is a lie and at other times it just may be a change in the client's financial position that they are not aware of. It will happen to us all at one time or another but there are ways to minimize the risk of this occurring.

First, I for one do not believe that clients misstate their financial or qualification status with intent to lie. I believe if you ask a client if they qualify for a purchase they are just going to say yes. This is especially true if they already own a home. In their mind, they have money in the bank and equity in a home so why wouldn't they qualify?

Good standard procedures mandate that before you start to show clients homes you make sure they have a prequalification letter from a lender. You have the right to see it. If they tell you, "Don't worry, I have it at home or in the office," tell them to send it to you when they return, and you can start showing homes as soon as you get it. If they still appear reluctant, you might want to consider thanking them for the opportunity to find their home but without a prequalification letter, you cannot serve their best interests.

Remember the colleague in your office who told you buyers were liars? When it came to that same situation, he continued without the prequalification letter and wasted his time with a client who was not qualified to buy.

At other times, the phrase is applied to situations other than financial qualifications. I recall an occasion where a husband and wife jointly owned their home. The wife lived in it with her son and daughter. The husband, according to the wife, was living out of the country where he had a business. When I took the listing, she said she had power of attorney to sign for her husband in order to list the house and presented a document showing that she did. But the document was in Creole and required a notarized translation. We were able to get the translation and list the house. However, when we went under contract, we required that the husband had to sign because the power of attorney only provided for listing the house and not selling it. That is where the truth failed to shine.

On the power of attorney, she had presented, there was the contact information of the notary in Port Au Prince. I called the notary and made an appointment for the husband to come in to sign an updated POA. I then gave the appointment information to the wife who started screaming at me, cursing me in English and Creole. Was there something wrong? Of course there was. I did not know it at the moment due to the wife's hysterical response but later I found out from another son who did not live in the house. His father had just died in prison and could not possibly have signed the first POA and certainly could not sign the updated one. This event demonstrated that both buyers and sellers can lie. So, my advice here is never to take a shortcut on appropriate administrative procedures. Never accept a document at face value if a document looks suspicious, make sure your title company can verify its authenticity.

Recounts of the incidents above collectively create a collage of human interactions that no real estate course can prepare you for. When you hear such stories, you usually think this can't possibly be true, but the fact is that these stories and any multitude of variations do happen every day. You need to be prepared to handle them when they occur. You can always walk away from the deal, but the bigger challenge is to try and navigate to a successful conclusion for the buyer, seller and yourself.

CHAPTER 15

Community Capture
The Most Important Marketing You Need To Succeed

When I became a Realtor I was already close to transitioning out of my community where my family and I had lived for 10 years. We first moved to a rental community until we found the perfect townhome in Cobblestone, a community of 778 townhomes and condominiums. It really was perfect, and my wife Gigi had no problem adding the finishing touches which made it distinctly ours.

I was still considered one of the new kids on the block in my brokerage and was in the process of trying to develop contacts from my sphere of influence when I realized a few things about my community and the possibilities it offered.

First, it was a gated community which did not allow door to door solicitation by other Realtors. So, no door knocking. That provided a hometown advantage to me because as the years would pass, I would come to have more face time with my neighbors. It also provided me with the opportunity to create in-house events and present myself to more of the community. I smelled opportunity right around the corner.

COMMUNITY CAPTURE STARTED WITH THE RESOURCE FAIR

When I acquired my townhome, the developer was

just getting ready to turn the association over to the community. There was a community meeting to elect the board of directors. Residents occupied completed units starting in 2007, but the first phase of the community sat without a board of directors until 2015 due to a pause in construction and the housing crash. Around that time, one condo and the HOA were voted in by the developer. When development started again, the Master Association was formed along with a second Condominium Association. I had a goal for this community: To be known as soon as possible by most of the residents and to make this community my prime sphere of influence and my legacy community where I would buy and sell homes to clients with whom I had a prior Real Estate relationship. The opportunity was presented to me at the first board meeting.

I was elected to the Townhome HOA. I had never held a position like that in any other community, and I was happy to be a member. During our first board meeting, the president asked each member to tell the board a little about themselves. And I, like the others, took my turn. When the meeting was over, the president approached me and asked me what I did as a producer in television and film, and I explained to her that I made things happen. She asked me if I could make something happen for the community and when I asked what she had in mind she told me she thought it might be a good idea if we had a resource fair. Many new owners were moving into the community and would certainly need to hire painters, carpenters, electricians, interior decorators, and all sorts of home fix up related companies. If I could bring a great selection of them together at the club house it would be a great community event. I told her I thought that I could do it and asked if she could give me a small budget for a few items that were already flying off the top of my head. I wanted to get a face painter for the kids because if the kids come the parents would come. I wanted to get some food trucks to come and I found out later I really did not need to pay them anything -- they just showed up without charging the community.

I had already decided prior to my election to the board to create a quarterly community magazine that would go to all 778 homeowners plus about 30 shops and restaurants in the plaza in front of the community. I could promote the fair in the first edition.

I was able to solicit small ads in the program. I charged between $50 and $200 to tout their product or services. The total production cost of a glossy 10-page magazine was around $1,100 including using Every Door Direct Postage (EDDM). I sold $1,400 worth of ads. The magazine had a few columns in it featuring the latest real estate news supplied by the Miami Board of Realtors specific to Southwest Broward County. It also had articles on real estate and mortgage trends. Both articles had my name and picture as the local real estate expert who was also a Cobblestone owner. There was also useful information for veterans, emergency phone numbers, school information and the resource fair, prominently featured on the front page.

At the time, there were several new restaurants opening in the plaza in front of Cobblestone and I invited them to take a free space at the fair and bring some of their food for residents to sample. They thought that was a really good idea and some of them, in the magazine as an example, offered a coupon for a discount off dinner for the evening they chose as their Cobblestone Family Night. Russo's Italian Restaurant took an ad and advertised "Monday is Cobblestone Night for Dinner at Russo's." At the first year's resource fair I had 38 vendors and nearly 400 residents showed up. Some of the vendors even provided giveaways that allowed me to create a drawing for attendees at the end of the event which was scheduled from 12:00 to 4:00 PM. The fair was an incredible success and the exposure that it provided was incalculable. The next year, I shot to the top of the list of realtors who were selling homes on the secondary market in Cobblestone. For the following three years we held the event and more sales developed. We stopped the resource fair due to Covid but in the future, we will pick up where we left off. However, missing a few years of the fair has not diminished my exposure in the community because of other marketing ideas I launched. Six years later, I am still the top realtor with nearly forty homes under contract. The closest Realtor last time I looked had sold six homes. There is no question that staging this event coupled with the on-going community magazine paved the road to success and will continue to build my legacy clientele..

In the years I added different types of vendors such as the YMCA that would set up free swimming lessons for the community children right before school let out in the summertime. Home Depot was a great contributor providing products and services ranging from air conditioners to electric to plumbing, all with a discount. And I am still doing the magazine to keep my name in front of the 778 homes.

This type of event in your community is something that you should consider. It can take a lot of work. It can be stressful. It can also make you king of the hill in your own backyard.

Another example of putting myself in front of the community comes every year at Halloween. I set up a table with a glowing pumpkin and a big orange Home Depot bucket filled with candy. I probably go through 25 pounds of candy every year and there is never any left over.

The Halloween Give Away

In our community, the homes participating in the Halloween festivities usually set up a table in front of their town home entrance and distribute candy to the children who circulate throughout the community. Cars do not drive on the main street so it is a safe fun time for everyone.

I also print out a small booklet with the floor plans of each home and insert the latest sale price and floor plan of each model. If the highest model was sold by The Fenster Group, that amount is highlighted. On the back two pages is the recipe for the world's greatest pumpkin pie. I asked Siri for a recipe, and she gave it to me. If you try it and it is not the world's greatest pie, file your complaint with Siri. Throughout the booklet is a never-ending collection of Halloween graphics.

When families come up to my table, I tell the children they can take as much candy as they can hold in one hand and then turn to the parents and as I hand them the Halloween booklet, I tell them "Do not be scared but your home valuation has just exploded." I then launch into a 30 second elevator pitch and move on to the next family. Personally, this is one of my favorite marketing events of the year.

The Emergency Contact Card

Of course, we all have business cards to hand out for every occasion but how many people keep them? I developed a card specific to my community. On the front of it is the traditional business card information. But on the back are emergency numbers that are useful for very many situations such as after hour HOA emergency contact numbers, police and fire to serpent and poison control. This is something people will want to keep around in a place they can find should they ever need it. Many people that I've worked with and talked to in the community always mention that they keep this card close at hand. It is the business card that keeps on doing business.

Mapping your Community

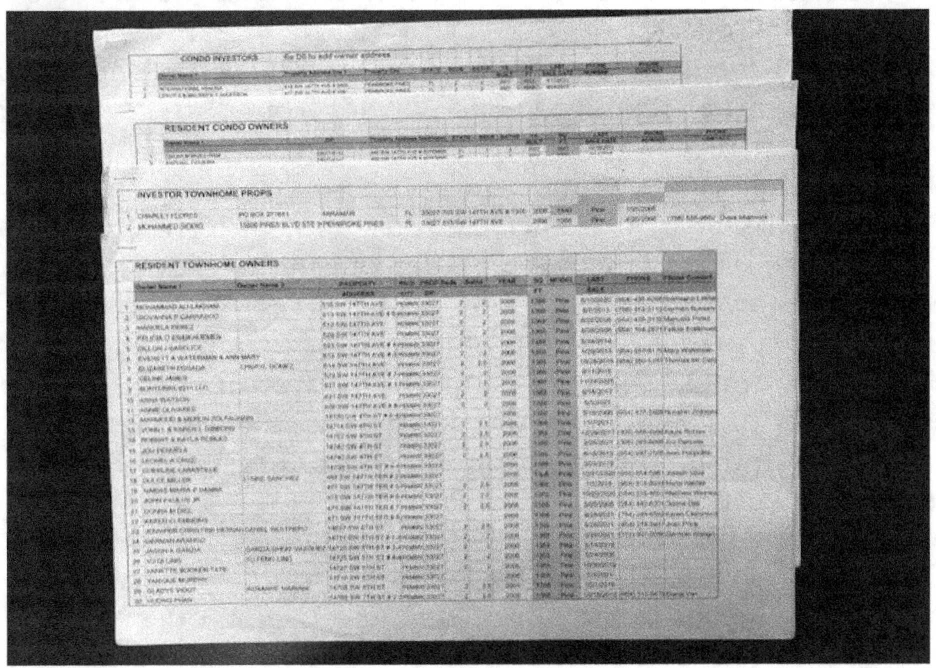

One of my other goals when I moved to Cobblestone was to create a map of the community. Not a geographical map but a data map. Regardless of where your Board of Realtors is, they are going to provide you with spreadsheet information on the sales and rentals in your community. Often the database is difficult to print out on one sheet because of the many columns of information. But you can download it to an Excel spreadsheet and then eliminate all the columns which are not useful information. You want to rearrange the columns in a manageable and easy to access order so that you can sort your database. How can you use this spreadsheet? You may have heard the saying that most buyers will sell their homes in eight to ten years. With the database organized by date of purchase, you can extract all those homes that fall in that 8-to-10-year range and then contact the owners via whatever method you determine. I prefer to write them personal letters and include an analysis of their home valuation. I use the Mini Sellers Report from RPR, Realtors Property Resource. Two days later, I follow up with a phone call.

Another resource I can extract from data mapping my community is to separate the homes owned and lived in by the owners and those occupied by tenants. Two months before each rental home is set to have the lease expire, the owner gets a call from me to see if he is going to renew the lease or if he wants to sell their home. I also keep a printed version of this database in my car so that every time I see a moving van in front of a home in my community, I check the address to see if it is a rental or sale and follow up with the owner to see if there is an opportunity.

The opportunities I have discussed and others that you can create specific to your community will not cost you a lot of money and they will bring you into face-to-face contact with future clients. I strongly recommend you put some thought into similar opportunities that are sustainable year after year at little cost.

My 24/7 Community Billboard

I love playing golf and spending a few hours with friends swiping golf balls and riding the hills of a golf course in a cart. On one trip, a young lady pulled up to our foursome with a golf cart laden with drinks. This was not so unusual because many golf courses provide this service but this time it was different. This golf cart had a small bulletin board hanging from the rear and on it were numerous business cards. A few of them were from Realtors. That was the missing element I needed to complete my community capture concept. I was going to get a cart and use it to promote The Fenster Group as the King of Cobblestone Real Estate.

My expectations were clear. If I did a mailing to my community, it was a one-time only event and I would never know how many people even read it. And of course it would cost me nearly $700. But my idea for the golf cart was constant. Every chance I had, I would ride the streets of the community and advertise my presence as the leading resident Realtor with more sales than the next five Realtors combined.

Weeks later, I had my golf cart with The Fenster Group and The Keyes Company decals.

The Fenster Group
Selling More Cobblestone Homes Than Any Other Realtor

Call For Free Home Valuation

754-224-7221

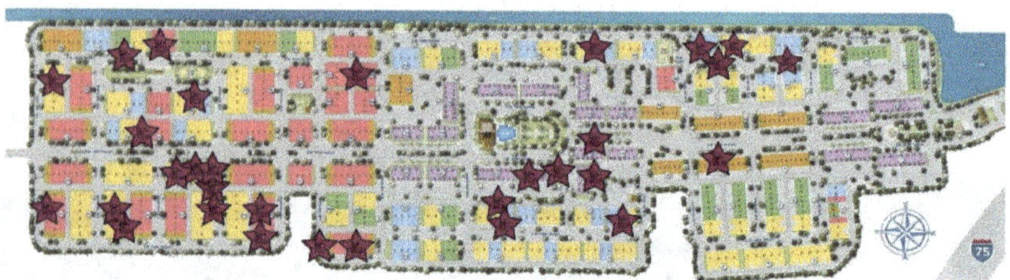

MORE THAN $14,000,000 SOLD

I also designed a sign which clearly showed my successful service to the homeowners in my community. I could change that sign at any time with more timely information updates such as Just Listed, Just Sold, and any other information I wanted to present. Later I added a rear hanging customizable sign which told viewers what type of home I was interested in selling i.e.

LOOKING TO BUY TAMARIND MODEL
OFFERING $650,000 or HIGHER
CALL YOUR COBBLESTONE REALTOR
RON FENSTER 754-224-7221

Everywhere I rode in the community, when I saw people on the sidewalks, I would wave at them, and they would wave back. Sometimes if I was searching for a particular property I would stop and ask if they were aware of any of their neighbor's intent to sell in the near future. A discussion would ensue, and I had established contact with another community member who did not personally know me.

From day one with the start of the Resource Fair promotion, I have been building my community capture program. The results are clear that I am the leading Realtor, not counting Realtors who worked for the developer during the initial sales period. The fact of the matter is that in my community I have sold nearly 40 homes with an average price of $400,000. In the past two years with values skyrocketing, the average home price has sold for $550,000. And with every passing year the number of sold units increases where I can see myself being able to slow down and continue to make a good income from just Cobblestone.

CHAPTER 16

Elbow Grease and Shoe Leather vs. Technology

As we look forward to the future of the real estate industry a question stares us right in the face. Will the application of the old work ethic of elbow grease and shoe leather provide your income or will the fog of technology engulf your efforts and create a false sense of security. Does it have to be one or the other? Or is there a way that both can exist in today's and tomorrow's real estate market?

Since the beginning of time, the necessity to make advances in industries across every profession has been created by the demand to break from the status quo and make improvements. At the same time these advances settled in, the door opened to obsolescence and extinction of certain jobs. But the door also stayed open for the birth of new and repurposed jobs. Real estate is by no means exempt from the lessons of history. Recall how things used to be prior to the age of the beeper, phone des, fax, cell phone, email, and computer. While there may be a tendency to be afraid of continuously advancing technology, especially for older realtors who learned to add using a pencil and paper, mastering today's technological skills did not always come easy.

I for one experienced this uneasiness in my prior businesses. When the video industry switched from an analog to a digital domain, the door opened to a rapidly advancing technology that changed the course and direction of the entertainment and advertising industries. In 1985 I founded Limelite Video, with a 15-

milliion dollar investment. It was a company created entirely in the digital domain specializing in video, graphics, and special effects. With roots in Miami, the instant success quickly spread to New York and LA. But with our success, the industry called for the next versions of hardware and software and within three years the company was being crushed and squeezed by the rapid introduction of newer technology. In three years, obsolescence was knocking at the gate.

Smaller desktop computers that were many times more powerful than their predecessors were flooding the market. Animation which had to be rendered out frame by frame was now being produced in real time. It was frightening for facility owners who were vested in old technology. But the old technology was just two to three years old. For those companies that were operating entirely in the current state-of-the-art, replacement technology had to be added to the menu of equipment offered to our clients. The (expensive) problem was that it competed with the more expensive technology which had not recouped its investment. Because the state-of-the-art never stayed still, development periods for technology that normally might take five years were now being introduced to the market in less than a year and the investment you had made became obsolete. In today's technology the computing power of an iPhone is many times more powerful than the largest computers I had purchased back then. Large facilities like mine with many employees were reduced to cubicles that could perform the same creative feats.

Having gone through that transformation in a prior career, I can draw on many parallels to the technology that is applied to today's real estate profession. And with the introduction of each new technological advancement, we have to ask ourselves how this is going to redefine our roles as realtors and the procedures we follow?

If you think about it, it would have been impossible 50 years ago to conduct a real estate transaction without the involvement of realtors and clients in face-to-face meetings. Think about real estate prior to the cell phone. It was not possible to talk to a client unless you were in your office or standing at a pay phone. Apart from an airport or large entertainment venue, when was the last time you saw a pay phone? And with the advent of the cell phone, lines of communication opened an entirely new reality for realtors. First, they were simply phones. Then advancements kicked in and phones became keyboards to faxes, emails, scanners, photography, video, contracts and social media.

Following the introduction of the cell phone came the laptop computer which no longer required a bevy of administrative assistants for every real estate office. Realtors could easily produce their own contracts and handle their correspondence. Once e-mail became an essential part of doing business, the industry took off at a speed that has not yet faltered. For the realtor, it was all a positive force with little or no downside. What could take hours now took minutes and it all could be monitored from your cell phone no matter where you were in the world.

With the introduction of computer applications that could address every facet of support and marketing services for realtors, everyone had the ability to become a one man show. And at that point the technological umbilical cord was severed and Realtors started to depart the Office Hive where they listened and learned and practiced their craft. The started to rely on a four-to-six-inch plastic and glass rectangle that they thought could provide them instant gratification for all things real estate. But can it really do that? The answer is yours to determine.

The next technological milestone stepping up to the

batter's box is Artificial Intelligence. The proponents of AI suggest that this could eradicate many of the functions a realtor currently provides to clients. But can it really? Can it do so with the accuracy and ethical considerations that are required by realtors in the service of their clients?

Looking back at the experience I personally witnessed during the 90s with my technology-based companies, I do not think so, at least for the foreseeable future. And here is my reasoning.

Technology might be able to fulfill Dale Carnegie's definition of sales: "Give your client enough information about your product and no more to convince him that he is justified in buying it." But can that same technology provide a client with the comfortable feeling of trust and confidence that a person provides? I say while AI may be the coolest thing, it cannot provide the secure confidence of a person who has gained your trust. Where can you look it in the eye? When your expectations fall short, who do you turn to for a better solution?

I cannot fathom a water cooler conversation between two realtors the day after a listing appointment or a contract signing which hands the success to AI over the knowledge and experience of a well-trained realtor. "And John, the beauty of this deal was that I never had to talk to my client or the buyer or the title company or the bank. As a matter of fact, this new software was so cool because I can't even recall my client's name."

Or, "Bob, I had the most incredible listing appointment yesterday. My new software package coupled with the X5Z10 Accelerated Thermal Cooled Chip on the Chat GPT version 644 absolutely convinced my clients they were justified in going with me over the competition."

"For sure, Bill. But the X5Z10 came on the market a few months ago and has been replaced by the X5Z10.5

Turbo Charged Zoom Acceleration Micro Real Estate Manager. It not only got me the listing, but it took me to contract before I even had a buyer."

Can future technology resolve conflicts between buyers and sellers that are common in the normal course of real estate transactions? Can the technology address and settle incidents of disagreement to the satisfaction of all parties? To be able to do so one would have to consider that humans agreed to surrender to whatever technology provided. And so, the fear of the realtor disappearing into oblivion is not a realistic view of the future.

Certainly, if there is a way to process, research, and expedite the steps of a real estate transaction, technology will and should find the means to do so. But to surrender to the concept that one day you may be replaced by a chip or Bot, is not a thing to fear.

The best advice I can provide, which is the same advice I apply in my business, is to embrace the new technologies with an understanding of their applications. Be selective and pick the ones that work for you and demonstrate they can advance your business. But never, ever, give in to the idea that the confidence and trust you can present as a professional realtor can be replaced by the next technological gizmo.

Be confident and continually educate yourself to new market trends. Always know that the door to a new client opens only because you convinced that client that they were justified in engaging your services.

Consider actor Michael Rennie in the classic 1950's science fiction film *The Day the Earth Stood Still*. Having landed his flying saucer in Washington, DC with the intention of making friends with earthlings he knew that human contact was the key to a successful transaction. He sent an earthling who had befriended him back to his craft which was being guarded by his technologically advanced robot, Gort. The ship was surrounded by the military and a crowd of citizens. The earthling relayed the message to the robot, memorializing those never to be forgotten sci-fi words *"Gort, Klatu Barato Nikto"* No one knows what those words meant for sure. But since his mission was to connect with earthlings and since flying saucers perhaps were not suitable for sustained housing it is not totally illogical to assume he might need to rent or buy and that he was asking Gort if he could find a good realtor in the crowd.